Human Services and Resource Networks

Rationale, Possibilities, and Public Policy

Seymour B. Sarason
Charles F. Carroll
Kenneth Maton
Saul Cohen
Elizabeth Lorentz

Human Services and Resource Networks

Jossey-Bass Publishers
San Francisco • Washington • London • 1977

HUMAN SERVICES AND RESOURCE NETWORKS
Rationale, Possibilities, and Public Policy
> by Seymour B. Sarason, Charles F. Carroll, Kenneth Maton,
> Saul Cohen, and Elizabeth Lorentz

FIRST EDITION

Code 7708

The Jossey-Bass
Behavioral Science Series

Preface

This book should be of interest to anyone concerned with human relationships, as they are affected by perception and definition of resources. This does not mean that we offer new insights and solutions. From our perspective, what we as authors have to say is literally quite obvious, but the obvious has a way of escaping sustained attention. Mired as they usually are in traditional ways of thinking, people note the obvious without pursuing its implications. "Of course," they say, "We know resources are not infinite and that man, anxious and adrift in the modern world, seeks the sense of rootedness." But when people look at proffered solutions, there is little or no evidence that either of these conditions is being taken seriously. And there certainly is no evidence that they are seen in their relationships to each other. If what we have to say has any claim to going beyond the obvious, it is from our emphasis on the relations between the need for community and the perception and definition of resources. It is an emphasis that pushed us to action, and so we describe, in the pages that follow, an attempt over three years to develop a network of individuals consistent with that emphasis. The leap from rationale to action is always sobering, but we are prepared for experiencing stubborn reality, because that reality reflects values and assumptions quite different from ours. We learned a great deal and accomplished more than we expected. In the minds and hands of others, more might have been learned and accomplished, and that assessment is not ritualistic obeisance to modesty. Our greatest satisfaction comes from the fact that, despite our limitations and errors, nothing in our experience contradicted the thrust of our rationale. Indeed, we recognized the possibility that we may not have taken that rationale as seriously as it deserves.

The authors are part of the cast of characters in the story we tell. There were many more, but, by agreement, they remain anonymous. This, unfortunately, is the case with the person we call Mrs. Dewar, who, it will be apparent, was the leading actor. We owe her much, not least for the fact that she graciously and unhesitatingly allowed us to describe her and her activities the way we saw them. Those from the community of Essex will be able to identify her. She deserves wider recognition.

The narrative portion of this book was written by Seymour B. Sarason and then critically reviewed by the other authors. Saul Cohen, as will become clear, played a conceptual-historical role, while Elizabeth Lorentz, a colleague of Sarason's, had responsibility for collecting and organizing observational material. The final draft was then prepared by Sarason. Chapters Ten and Eleven, the review of the literature, represented several months of intensive labor by Charles Carroll, Kenneth Maton, and Stefan Presser. Carroll and Maton had the responsibility for writing up this fascinating, emerging, sprawling, and disconnected literature.

The work contained herein was developed with partial support from the Group on School Capacity for Problem Solving of the National Institute of Education, Department of Health, Education, and Welfare (Order No. NIE–P–76–0325). The opinions expressed in this document do not necessarily reflect the position of the National Institute of Education, and no official endorsement should be inferred.

We are grateful to Eleanor Smith, who typed the different drafts and somehow managed to bear with us through a difficult period.

New Haven, Connecticut   SEYMOUR B. SARASON
February 1977

Contents

The Authors

Seymour Sarason is professor of psychology and I.B.M. Professor of Urban Education at Yale University. He founded, in 1962, and directed, until 1970, the Yale Psycho-Educational Clinic, one of the first research and training sites in community psychology. He has received awards from the divisions of clinical and community psychology, as well as two awards from the American Association on Mental Deficiency. He is the author of numerous books and articles and has made contributions in such fields as mental retardation, culture and personality, projective techniques, teacher training, the school culture, and anxiety in children. His last two books, *The Creation of Settings and the Future Societies* and *The Psychological Sense of Community* (Jossey-Bass, 1972 and 1974), contain themes that are elaborated on in the present volume.

Charles F. Carroll, Kenneth Maton, and Elizabeth Lorentz are research colleagues of Sarason's. They have been involved in various community psychology efforts, one of which was the Essex network. Carroll is finishing his doctorate at Yale, and Maton is pursuing his at the University of Illinois at Urbana. Lorentz has successfully resisted efforts urging her to seek graduate degrees.

Saul B. Cohen is director of the Graduate School of Geography at Clark University and has long been concerned with network concepts that are central not only to his discipline but to the larger society as well. He has been a frequent research contributor to his field. Beginning in the sixties, he played an influential role in federal efforts to develop new types of networks that would make more permeable the boundaries between schools and their social surroundings. Cohen was responsible for developing the Tri-University Network (Clark, Yale, Stony Brook) that later interconnected with the Essex network described in this book. His most recent book is *Experiencing the Environment* coauthored with Seymour Wapner and Bernard Kaplan.

Human Services and Resource Networks

Rationale, Possibilities, and Public Policy

1

Human Resources and Social Networks

ଧ୍ଧାଧାଧାଧାଧାଧାଧାଧାଧାଧାଧାଧାଧାଧ

W orld War II and its aftermath
took the concept of "one world" out of the realm of rhetoric
and apparent utopian idealism and placed it in the daily lives of
people. We know, as man has never known before, that our individual lives can be altered by people and events, near and far. It
is ironic that we have reached this world view, which some
individuals over the centuries dreamed about and longed for, with
foreboding as well as nostalgia for the past. Unprecedented interrelatedness has been accepted more as a fact than as a value, because the consequences of interrelatedness conflict with traditional
modes of organization and their underlying values. There is a part
of each of us that knows how inescapably interrelated and interdependent our world has become, but there is another part that
feels impotent and puzzled about how to salvage our individualities
as we see ourselves caught in a world net the strands of which seem

1

endless, endlessly strong, and ever growing. If people have accepted the ideas of one world, it has not prevented them from characterizing that world in quite dysphoric terms.

This book is not about the world but about a set of problems, quite circumscribed in scope and place, that nevertheless indirectly derives from that complex of forces and events requiring people to accept and struggle with the fact that we live in an interconnected world. That we, the authors, like so many other people, found ourselves thinking in terms of the concept of network was not because we woke up to the fact of interrelatedness. Awareness of that fact has always been part of people's perceptions. If we were thinking of networks, it was because we were forced to by the obvious disjunction between the quality and quantity of interrelatedness, on the one hand, and people's needs and goals, on the other hand. But the perception of that disjunction became sharper as individual and societal efforts to erase that disjunction were minimally successful. The turbulent sixties parented the cynical seventies. As we reflected about our own experiences in relation to efforts to cope with this disjunction, we came to see that we had glossed over examining the relationships between two factors: the fact that resources are always limited, and that people hungered for a more substantial feeling of community. The second factor has been recognized and commented on for centuries, but the first factor has only in recent years received reluctant attention and recognition. Our reflections led us to the conclusion that it would not be until people accepted the fact of limited resources—not until they saw that to achieve their goals would require them to exchange resources in barter style with others who had some of the resources they needed—that they stood a chance of experiencing a more satisfying sense of community. It was not only that people needed each other in a psychological sense, but they also needed each other to achieve their goals in work. The two needs had to be seen as different sides of the same coin of living.

This book is a description of a three-year project to develop and sustain a network of very diverse people in their efforts "to use" each other in ways that furthered them in their goals of work, at the same time that a sense of bondedness was enhanced. They were people of very different backgrounds, agency affiliation, work roles, status, age, and perspective. They did not come and stay together because there was money to be allocated. Indeed, it was made clear from the start that the purpose of the network was to figure out how we could mutually contribute to each other's resource needs through ideas and resource exchange. And, if we did not possess the resources a member needed, how could we use the other networks of which we were a part to help the person secure those resources? Resource exchange would always be a two-way street; that is, it had to be mutually enhancing. Any resource need was not a problem, but an opportunity to use existing resources in more effective, personally productive ways.

In recent years, the word *network* has become part of common parlance. Rarely is the word used with intended precision, but rather as a label reflecting the obvious fact that each person has a wide array of relationships, the bases of which can vary in the extreme. Each of us knows, has met, and has had commerce with countless people, but what the label *network* ordinarily suggests is that with a portion of these people we have a relationship permitting us to "approach" them. And we may approach them with the deliberate aim of asking them to help us establish a similar relationship with a person we do not know. We are usually unaware both of the extent and basis of these relationships until events force that knowledge on us. The purpose of the Essex network was to demonstrate that this awareness can be considerably expanded with productive consequences.

The organization of this book presented several major problems. The first of these had to do with the relationship of our efforts to the ever growing but scattered literature on networks. The truth is that when we began to develop the Essex network we were aware that "networks" and "networking" were in the air, so to speak, and that some seminal publications (for example, see Schön, 1971) were beginning, as we were, to try to clarify the issues and possibilities. The literature we were aware of did not directly influence our actions, but it supported us in the belief that what we wanted to learn on the level of action could be personally productive and, perhaps, conceptually important. Shortly after the Essex network had become a reality, we undertook the literature review, but we had no expectation that it would take us into many disciplines, each of which seemed not to know what was developing in the others. Indeed, it took us into disciplines (for example, mathematics, some branches of economics) beyond our competence. What was so impressive was how a concept of networks began to become visible and important in so many disciplines after World War II. This, surely, was not fortuitous, but neither was a simple answer at hand. We decided to organize a literature review and to include those publications that seemed most relevant and comprehensible to social scientists generally. We have no doubt that over the next decade interest in and research on concepts of networks will greatly increase. (It is more than a straw in the wind that a special section on the study and implementation of networks has been created in the National Institute of Education.) Because of the characteristics of the literature, we decided not to begin this book with the customary review of the literature. To weave this literature review into the narrative of the Essex network would have placed great strains on the reader, aside from doing an injustice both to our story and the literature. Consequently, we have placed the literature toward the end of the book (Chapters Ten and Eleven), indicating there points of conceptual contact between the Essex network and the research literature. In Chapter Two, we begin with a very brief overview of the literature and move on to the rationale that gave rise to the Essex network.

The second major problem had to do with the scope and depth of description. How much detail can the reader absorb, especially since the cast of characters is not small and, more important, since each character is part of many and diverse types of networks? Take, for example, Mrs. Dewar, who was the moving force in the Essex network. To understand how this remarkable person came to her ideas about resource exchange and how she helped to organize the Essex network would require an overwhelming amount of detailed description composed of biography and American history. Even leaving such a description aside, we were still left with the fact that a blow-by-blow account of how the network developed (of how *any* network develops) confronts one with an ever-growing list of people, places, and agencies directly and indirectly linked to each other. One is reminded of those complicated anthropological charts and descriptions of kinship relationships that certainly convey the complexity of interrelatedness, at the same time that they overwhelm our capacity cognitively to grasp, let alone remember, what is presented to us. The problem of description became less thorny when we realized that what was distinctive about the Essex network was not complexity of interrelatedness and detail (that complexity is and increasingly will be a characteristic of networks), but its rationale. However, in order to give the reader some idea of what people in the Essex network "do" and how the network grows, we present, in Chapter Three, brief skeleton descriptions in a time-sequence form of several "doings."

Chapter Four focuses on the three individuals: how and why they came together and the process they had to go through to arrive at a common perspective and the decision to develop an action network consistent with the underlying rationale. This was no easy process. For a period of months, the Essex network was an idea in search of an opportunity for implementation. The last half of that chapter describes a fateful meeting from which the Essex network grew rapidly. The meeting was fateful not only for its consequences but also for what it taught us about how to think about and prepare for network meetings.

The quality, substance, and ambience of network meetings are crucial for an understanding of the Essex network. John Dewey once said that school is not a preparation for life—it is life. Similarly, network meetings are the most important test of how well theory and practice are wedded. We pursue this matter in Chapter Five in order to emphasize how the growth of the network presented some knotty problems about how to capitalize in these meetings on the different activities that went on between these meetings. In Chapter Five, we also describe how the Essex network interconnected with one other network in a truly mutually rewarding way. We could have used other networks to illustrate how interconnections came about, but we chose the triuniversity network because it was a deliberate attempt to make sense out of a long series of largely unsuccessful efforts in the Office of Education to forge networks that would lead to the improvements in American education. These were efforts spearheaded by Donald Bigelow and no one knew better than he why the concept of networks was crucial, just as no one saw better than he why his efforts would, at best, be minimally successful. From the standpoint of intellectual history, neither the Essex nor the triuniversity network is comprehensible without some attention to Bigelow's efforts.

In Chapter Six, we pursue the functions and purposes of the general meeting, but now from the standpoint of the mixed blessings of growth. The fact is that the Essex network grew so rapidly and was involved in so many activities that no one person could coordinate or even know about all that was going on. From the standpoint of the sense of common origins and of the sense of community, one could question the desirability of such growth. After all, the Essex network was not developed to replicate the unhealthy state of affairs in which individuals and agencies were unknown to or unavailable to each other. One of the immediate consequences of the growth was the recognition that the general meetings were in danger of losing or diluting their centripetal function. How we coped with this problem is discussed in Chapter Six.

Chapter Seven takes up the issues of leadership and funding, and, in the case of the Essex network, that means focusing on Mrs. Dewar. These issues can be put in this question: To what extent is the Essex network the result of the efforts of atypical people, particularly someone as atypical as the person we have named Mrs. Dewar? If the answer is "To a great extent," the Essex network has little general significance. In Chapters Seven and Eight we confront this question. If we conclude, as we do, that this kind of answer is not warranted, it is because our experience indicated that what kept the Essex network going and growing was less Mrs. Dewar's status and influence than it was her contribution to the network's rationale, which seemed to strike a very responsive chord in almost all of the people in or affected by the Essex network. Chapter Eight, in particular, argues that one does not have to be a Mrs. Dewar to develop a barter type of network. The galvanizing force is in the realm of ideas and values, and once these are coherently articulated, the obstacles to implementation do not disappear—but neither do they demand a Mrs. Dewar to be overcome. We by no means rule out the possibility that other people can implement the rationale far more consistently than was done by those leading or part of the Essex network. We do not present the Essex network as a success story, because success in this world is almost always partial, transient, and often illusory. At this stage in our experience, we feel increasingly secure about the thrust of our rationale, and the story we tell is for the purpose of stimulating others who can go beyond us.

A final word about the organization and substance of this book, and it is about our emphasis in the rationale on the necessity to join the fact of limited resources with the psychological sense of community as a value informing action. This necessity is easy to state and justify. It is relatively easy to get agreement on a value, especially if it is one that seems to put you on the side of unalloyed virtue. However, between values and action is a field of mines that far more often than not absorbs one in the pressures and ambiguities of action at the expense of appropriate concern for the values initially giving rise to actions. We were very sensitive to this possibility, not because we thought we could successfully and completely avoid inconsistencies, but because we did not want to deceive ourselves and, later, our readers. Therefore, in our narrative we have deliberately narrowed the range of description of the activities of the Essex network, and we have concentrated on those activities and procedures (like meetings) that best illuminate and test our rationale. So there is much in our narrative about "the general network meeting" and "meetings between meetings," because the quality or ambience of these meetings will tell the reader more about our consistency in action with our rationale than will parading the extent of the network's quantitative growth. It is more important that the reader understand the significance of these meetings, and the problems involved in preparing for and running them, than that he trace in minute detail what are easiest to describe: overt activities and their interrelationships. For example, we deleted from our narrative a chapter containing verbal and graphic descriptions of the growth of the Essex network. It was quite an impressive chapter in much the same way that a Rube Goldberg cartoon is impressive, wheels within wheels seemingly going in the same and different directions at the same time, and proving to the reader that there is a fine line between order and chaos. We deleted that chapter not only because of the overwhelming and confusing detail it contained, but also because it emphasized what the reader already knows or will quickly grasp: Each of us is part of intricate networks, and if one sets one's mind, as we did, to enlarging the size and geographical range of those networks, the task of listing and describing those enlargements is formidable in the extreme. What is far from obvious are the different values informing different networks, and that is why the organization and thrust of our narrative emphasizes our rationale. This rationale is not unique to the Essex network. Undoubtedly, both now and in the past, in this as well as in other societies, there have been networks based on the perception of the need to relate limited resources to the need for the sense of community. (The history of communes, for example, goes back a long way, and in many of them, aspects of our rationale were present.) We make no claim to uniqueness insofar as rationale is concerned. However, it is our belief and hope that in describing the Essex network we will be bringing to the attention of others issues and possibilities that are at the heart of the dilemmas of modern living.

2

Rationale
of Social Networks

The word *network* has been used in more than a dozen fields, including sociology, anthropology, psychiatry, psychology, administrative sciences, geography, city planning, and communications engineering. Although there is little cross-indexing among fields, *network* has surprisingly similar but not identical meanings across these disciplines, each discipline emphasizing different points, and certainly various disciplines studying dissimilar phenomena. Most usages are not mutually exclusive and reflect the same underlying idea, that is, that each person or organization has a wide array of interrelationships, the bases of which can vary in the extreme.

This sprawling literature is organized and reviewed in Chapters Ten and Eleven. Most of this book is about a particular network, the Essex network. However, it appeared that it would be helpful at the start for the reader to know major meanings of

9

network, for at least two reasons. First, since the word *network* is part of common parlance, many readers may know a particular meaning for it and should be alerted to other uses of the term. Second, throughout the discussion of the Essex network, the term is used with various emphases that are similar to the variations in the literature.

One might first ask why so many disciplines have developed a network concept with similar meanings. When one reviews the literature on network, one is struck by how much the use of this concept is a post-World War II phenomenon. This does not mean that the presence of network structures in society is so recent; indeed, the origins are far in the past, particularly with the social and technological changes of the industrial revolution; for example, telephone lines criss-crossed the country and made interrelating much easier, and often necessary for competitive survival. There can be no doubt that the relatively recent development of network research is a reflection of the recognition of a change in world view that has seeped into the minds of people everywhere. It is commonplace to say we live in "one world": that any one person, organization, or community is so interrelated with many other elements in the world as to interconnect everybody in a small world both technologically and interpersonally. Such pervasive interrelatedness is the basic element that the meanings of network reviewed here have in common. Because no one can look at the totality of one world (the "total network"), various researchers have been forced to focus on or emphasize particular aspects for investigation.

The first type of usage is to provide a *structural* description of the interrelated world. The network image connotes an interrelatedness composed of (1) direct linkages of any one unit with certain other units and (2) indirect linkages of any one unit with many other units attached by chains of linkages. By definition, only one person or organization is chosen as the means by which to demonstrate interrelatedness with other units in the network. However, a highly "dense" network is one where many of the individuals also know each other, and density has been shown to have major effects on individuals (for example, see Bott, 1957). With few exceptions of totally isolated individuals or organizations, the total network, including all potential and indirect interrelationships (for example, friends of friends of friends, and so on), ultimately encompasses the entire world. However, in order to have a discrete structure that is possible to study, social scientists have focused on the linkages of one person or organization with other such units. The focal unit has often been termed the *ego*. Other such units that have direct or indirect linkages with the ego are part of the ego's network. This network has often been called an *individual's total network*, and has fairly unlimited possibilities. For example, if one thinks about a mayor's total network, the number of people with direct or indirect ties to this person through personal and political contacts can be huge. Nevertheless, this structure of ego-centered networks has typically been helpful in defining a subject for study (for example, see Barnes, 1954; Shulman, 1972; Curtis and Zurcher, 1973). Another structure, a mesh network, which interorganizational researchers have found especially useful (for example, Turk, 1970), again includes only part of a total network, but without reference to only one organization. (Only a few researchers have actually used the term *mesh network*, though others have described networks that follow the definition of a mesh network, and this term will be used in this chapter to refer to all such uses of the term *network*.) The mesh image connotes a number of organizations interacting with each other, including direct and indirect ties. The limiting criterion may be geographic or a particular common function. In sum, whether scientists thought of the total network, focused on an ego-centered network, or focused on a mesh network, these terms have been used to define structures common in today's world.

Scientists further focused on networks by considering the nature of the *interactions* among units in an ego-centered or a mesh network. The most important idea is the "partial network" or "action set," in which an ego-centered network is limited on the basis that the individuals serve a particular function for the ego; for example, getting elected to public office (Mayer, 1962, 1966). In this example, the ego typically actively calls on members of this partial network to perform certain functions concerned with the ego's election. A characteristic of interactions within this type of interactional network is that some sort of exchange, or reciprocity, takes place; for example, services are given by one person in return for political favors by the other, services are given for money, services are given for friendship, friendship is given for friendship, and so on. The many ways in which a politician can pay back members of his network are unimportant, however, for the definition of this network, which is simply in terms of the persons the politician has call on to help in his election.

Another type of ego-centered partial network is the supportive one, in which the ego is relatively passive in the interaction, and the network is defined by a certain type of influence on or support for an individual. For example, one might study the network that influences a person migrating from country to city, or the network of support around a hospitalized cardiac patient (Croog, Lipson, and Levine, 1972). The ego may reciprocate for the support; for example, the cardiac patient may write thank-you notes, or help the son of a friend find a job years later. However, this half of generally reciprocal interactions is unimportant for the definition of this network, which is simply based on influence on or support of the ego.

One type of partial network is a mesh where many individuals are likely to know each other, for example, in an extended family, where certain family members choose to interact with each other (Sussman and Burchinal, 1962), in a series of communal houses in a geographic location (Speck, Barr, Eisenman, Foulks, Goldman, and Lincoln, 1972), or in a series of individuals from organizations in a locality who come together by choice for mutual benefits around common interests. There is typically a strong sense of call among units and a sense of community is felt by participants, whereas, by definition, in an ego-centered network only the ego necessarily interacts with, has call on, or is supported by the others in the network.

Another type of mesh partial network is one through which new ideas or cultural norms diffuse, for example, the diffusion of a scientific finding (for example, see Coleman, Katz, and Menzel, 1957) or the spread of gossip, (for example, see Epstein, 1961). The thing diffused, plus perhaps geography, tend to define the limits of this mesh partial network. It is a mesh in that the source of the original stimulus cannot be determined and in that it is not activated by and does not affect one individual or organization in particular.

Finally, researchers have discussed a certain type of intra-organizational relationship within an organization described as a "network structure of control, authority, and communication" (Burns and Stalker, 1961). Specifically, such an organization would have more flexible and less hierarchical authority or control structures and a lateral rather than vertical direction of intraorganizational communication, with information input into diverse points in the organization. Individuals would have significant reciprocal relationships with diverse others who span traditional, narrowly defined, functionally specific role, group, and system categorizations. Again, it is the nature of the interactions among interrelated units that defines this as a network.

In sum, to conceptualize interrelatedness in the world researchers have developed several overlapping definitions of a network: (1) a structural definition involving, ultimately, the total world, ego-centered interrelationships, or mesh interrelationships; (2) partial networks or action sets defined by a function served by persons for an ego; (3) influence or support partial networks defined by effects on a relatively passive ego; (4) mesh networks consisting of individuals who choose to interrelate around family ties or other common interests; (5) mesh networks for diffusion of innovations or cultural norms; and (6) nonhierarchical, flexible relationships within an organization characterized by lateral communication and information input into diverse points. In all but the first definition, the type of interaction among units is the major defining characteristic. While reciprocity is usually present, the character of one direction of the interaction often defines the network type. Differing sense of call or types of influence are important characteristics of interactions for defining types of networks.

There is also a body of literature concerned with attempts to intervene in networks to achieve specified ends. In many cases, interveners have sought to activate networks that existed but were dormant due to lack of conceptualizing them or unwillingness to activate them on the part of the ego. For example, Speck (1967) assembled family, neighbors, and friends of an adolescent schizophrenic person to solve problems and to provide resources and support for the troubled person. Speck became a leader in this network, although subtly he was both insider and outsider. Throughout this literature, interveners have had an implicit recognition of the absence of a sense of community and have sought to establish it through networks that already existed in potential.

Although the research literature lends itself to categorization of types of networks, typologies too frequently and prematurely emphasize differences rather than communalities and somewhat arbitrarily (and unwittingly) do violence to the social complexities they seek to illuminate. In developing the Essex network, and in organizing our thoughts and experiences in order to describe it, we were not concerned with the question of the type of network Essex was but rather with its rationale, problems, and outcomes. We knew that our interest in networks was a reflection of a burgeoning interest of many people in our society, many of whom had very practical, day-to-day goals, in contrast to scientific researchers, whose quest is for generality and explanation. We had both practical and scientific interests in networks, but we assumed that our scientific interests would be more productively furthered by a sustained practical effort to implement our ideas. We did not want "to study," but rather to experience networks. And we did not want to experience just any network, but rather one based on a rather clear set of considerations.

In the remainder of this chapter, we will discuss some of the considerations and experiences that led us to see the concept of networks as central to our thinking and required us to try to gain clarity about its conceptual characteristics. It would be more correct to say that we came to see that the failure, absolute or relative, of most programs in human services (and the resulting cynicism about mounting any successful program) was in large measure due to unexamined, oversimple, and invalid conceptions of the nature, extent, and bases of human interrelationships. One needs neither theory nor research to know that each of us is part of many kinds of social networks, or that to accomplish the objectives of a program requires that you take some account of the types and extent of these networks in order to maximize resources available to the program. Such knowledge, however, has not been productive in practice. On the contrary, it has frequently happened that in the course of program development and implementation, resources have shrunk and the scope and quality of relationships within and among social networks have deteriorated. We do not claim that this frequent state of affairs is due only to an inadequate conceptualization of human networks, but we will argue and attempt to demonstrate that recognizing and correcting this inadequacy explains a good deal about past failures and provides a foundation for more successful future efforts.

In presenting the considerations and experiences that gave centrality in our thinking to the concept of networks, the "story" will sound more rational than in fact it was. For one thing, each of the writers came to the concept independent of the others and from widely differing backgrounds and experiences. Initially, we did not come together to study networks, but rather to explore the possibility that each of us could use each other for a particular programatic purpose. At that early point, each of us sensed the importance of the network concept, but it was not until each participated in the others' network that we recognized the necessity to organize our past and present experiences: to put into words much that was common but implicit in our thinking. We did not undertake the task for our benefit alone, although that was important, but rather because of dissatisfaction (ours and others') with our answers to questions about how and why we were part of a large, active network (and interrelationships of networks) composed of a wide array of individuals and agencies who were sharing resources in mutually productive ways, with no exchange of money. Rightly or wrongly, our networks impressed a lot of people who found it hard to understand how the networks were sustained in light of their informal structure and the apparent "planned" unpredictability of their future directions. The questions were many, and although we could describe our activities, we early learned that what we were glossing over were some bedrock considerations without which the description of our activity could only elicit bewilderment and even disbelief. We turn now to these considerations.

Limited Resources

It is axiomatic in economics that resources are limited. This may long have been obvious to economists, but it was not so to the general public or even to most sophisticated people in other disciplines. In recent decades, the axiom has gained wide currency, although in very selected ways. In regard to many of our most needed natural resources, we have been forced to recognize the cogency of the axiom. In the realm of human affairs, the implications of the axiom are hardly sensed. Let us pursue this question: How many more physicians would be needed to give adequate medical care to all in our society? We can safely assume that there would be controversy about defining adequate care, but it is also safe to assume there would be general (but no unanimous) agreement that many more physicians would be required.[1] Whether the increase would be of the order of 25, or 50, or 100 percent, the absolute number of new physicians would run into the thousands. These numbers could not be trained without creating a few score of

[1] That one can count on controversy about defining adequate care (and, therefore, the number of physicians needed) is seen in a report (*New York Times,* September 3, 1976) by the Carnegie Council on Policy Studies in Higher Education, asserting that new medical schools are unnecessary, foreign doctors receive inferior medical education, and that existing medical schools can educate all the physicians needed in this country. At the same time, the council notes that the ratio of physicians to population is least favorable in the East, South Central and West South Central states, as well as in ghetto areas of the nation's large urban centers. Since the council's report does not hold out much hope that these areas will receive more and better medical care in the future, it is strange that the council does not entertain the possibility that by training more physicians, thereby introducing more competition, these areas may become more attractive to physicians. In any event, the American Medical Association immediately took exception to the council report. If our own observations of people's perception of physicians as too busy, too inaccessible, and immorally expensive have any merit, the council's report will be seen as having an Alice-in-Wonderland flavor. How a problem is defined and whose ox is gored are, of course, highly correlated processes.

   It really makes little difference what professional groups we used to illustrate our points, especially because we are primarily interested in professionals in human services who, generally speaking, emphasize the discrepancy between the needs of people and the number of professionals available to deal with these needs. As we discuss in the next section ("The Universal Complaint"), we have never known a professional or human service agency who felt that it had sufficient resources to meet people's needs as defined by professionals. And, as we shall see, in practice the most crucial determinant of the degree of the discrepancy between supply and demand is how and by whom the problem is defined. Someone once said that one of the diseases of professionalism is the tendency to define a problem in a way so as to require only professionals for its solution, thereby rendering the problem unsolvable. It is a tendency as socially self-defeating as it is well intentioned.

new medical schools, the cost of which would run into billions of dollars. If our society were to go that route, several problems would have to be confronted. Where would one get the personnel to man these new facilities? It could be argued that existing medical schools vary tremendously in quality, in part because the number of truly first-rate physicians is small and in part because only a few medical schools have the traditions, atmosphere, and resources to attract and keep first-rate faculty. As a consequence, it would be argued, there is a concentration of such faculty in relatively few centers, and the bulk of medical schools must settle for less able people and, therefore, their students are less well prepared to give adequate care. So, if you create twenty new medical schools, the competition for scarce quality personnel could intensify with at least two possible results: The quality of the best medical schools would be diluted (they are brought closer to the mean), or the new medical schools will be unable to compete "in the market" and they will settle for second best. This line of argument could be much more developed and it is one guaranteed to arouse violent differences of opinion. But everyone would agree that quality of medical personnel was not uniform and, indeed, there is no evidence to suggest that the distribution of quality is other than a normal one; that is, a small percentage would be excellent, an equal percentage would be poor, and the bulk of personnel would be bunched somewhat above *and* below the group mean. Quality is a limited resource, and to plan as if it were in large supply is to deny reality.

One could counter this argument by saying that training physicians to give adequate care does not require a largely first-rate faculty, who for the most part are more interested in research than they are in teaching for practice. What is required are good teachers, and although they are not an unlimited resource, there are more of them than there are first-rate medical faculty and researchers. Furthermore, this argument could continue, even if the first argument had some validity, there are so many people receiving no or scandalously poor medical care that they would benefit immensely from the increase in the number of physicians who, although not receiving the highest quality of medical training, would nevertheless be far better than no service at all. The major task is to increase the number of good teachers. This argument, like the opposing one, assumes that the quality necessary for a desirable outcome is limited. Unfortunately, in the heat of controversy in which the proponents of one position try to demolish the proponents of the other position, both manage to overlook their area of agreement: The quality of human resource considered by each to be desirable and necessary is in short supply. And by overlooking this agreement, they no longer are in a position to confront the implications of a major obstacle to a desirable outcome.

But let us assume there is no controversy and everyone agrees that we need more physicians, more medical schools, and the only obstacle to overcome is finding the additional billions per year such an expansion would cost. Can we afford to do it? There are those who would say that the more appropriate question is, How can we justify not doing it? That is to say, the problem is at root a moral one and, when seen in that way, what is required is an act of national will and the problem will be solved. Some who take this stance would maintain that, given our riches as a country, we could mount such a program without taking away resources from other programs. (This is like in the sixties, when some people said we could afford to go to the moon and conduct the war on poverty at the same time we were conducting a foreign war.) By formulating the solution in moral terms, the assumption about adequacy of resources goes unexamined. Furthermore, this moral stance about a particular program glosses over the fact that other people take a similar stance about other programs. Moral stances are not in short supply and when one arrays the programs to which such stances give rise, the assumption of unlimited resources is seen for what it is: an uncritically accepted assumption.

When proponents of a new program confront the reality of limited resources, they accept (or are forced to accept) a scaling down of their plans. So, instead of twenty new medical schools, they may be willing to settle for five, hoping that in the future they will gain new resources. After all, five does represent an incremental gain, even though the discrepancy between what needs to be done and will be done is still large. Morality has, so to speak, won a battle in a long war. But this sense of satisfaction is based on the assumption that available resources will either remain constant or increase. What if available resources decline or the competition for existing resources becomes more fierce because new needs arise from within or without our society? Anyone familiar with our history knows that our economy has long had the characteristics of a yo-yo. And anyone familiar with recent international history knows the degree to which the definition of the scope of our society's resources has become dependent on what happens elsewhere in the world. Therefore, to assume that resources available to us will be constant or increase is, to say the least, dangerous. Yet that assumption has been given a wide degree of acceptance. The exposure in practice of its invalidity has caused widespread disappointment and even cynicism, but, unfortunately, there continues to be a resistance to the idea that among the reasons for program failure or inadequacy, the assumption of unlimited or increasing resources occupies an important place.

The size of available resources to deal with any social problem is a function of many factors, but certainly one of the most important is how the problem is defined. For example, in presenting the problem of providing adequate medical care, the problem was defined in a way so that its solution *required* training many more physicians. *Such a definition contains the "solution," but, as we tried to demonstrate, it is a solution that renders the problem unsolvable.* Put in another way, resources are always limited, but the discrepancy between what needs to be done and resources available to do it is frequently widened by our definition of what needs to be done.

The Universal Complaint

We have never known of a human service agency of any kind that asserted that it had the resources to accomplish its goals. That is to say, the demand for the agency's services always exceeds what the agency feels it can and should supply. The solution, far more often than not, is put in terms of obtaining more money to hire more staff. Occasionally, it is put not in terms of money but of being unable to locate and attract personnel who are in known short supply. However it is put, it always reflects a concept of "the market," in which it is competing for limited resources. Put in another way, the agency defines resources as those it can purchase and, therefore, control and distribute, consistent with its definition of its task. The agency usually knows where the additional resources are located, but unless it has the funds to purchase them (in whole or in part), the resources do not, so to speak, exist.

One of us (Seymour B. Sarason) has illustrated this point, and we give in the following quote that part of the discussion most relevant to our present purposes: What the reader needs to know is that a plan was devised whereby university faculty and graduate and undergraduate students would set up, without cost, a department of psychology in a high school.

> Several school systems were quite eager for us to use their high schools. Although we monotonously repeated that there was a fair chance that we would fall on our faces, that we did not view ourselves as experts in high school teaching, that graduate and even (highly selected) undergraduates would be involved in addition to faculty, that we did not want to be viewed as in any way imping-ing on any one else's territory—the response was uniformly enthusiastic and for two reasons. First, in each school system there were some personnel who asserted that I was a responsible individual who knew something about schools. Second, they said they had so many unmotivated students, and since psychology was intrinsically fasci-nating to everybody (they obviously never sampled un-dergraduate opinion!), they could only see our involve-ment as helpful. In essence, we had no "port of entry problem" to speak of. The fact that we posed no credentialing issues was also a plus. The project lasted one year and could not be continued because of a variety of serious illnesses in my family that made planning and commitment an exercise in futility. The school was eager for us to continue. Not only was the teaching perceived as successful, but in diverse ways our group became in-volved with different individuals, groups, and depart-ments in ways that we had hoped for and that were regarded by school personnel as extremely helpful in achieving desired changes.
>
> And now for the major point: *We came to the schools. We offered certain services and a long range*

plan which the schools saw as a possible help to a serious problem. It never occurred to them to come to us. Given their accustomed way of viewing the community, it could not occur to them that perhaps they had a "right" to request and even to demand help. They viewed the problems with which they were faced as their responsibility, solvable either by existing resources or additional ones they could buy (knowing full well that they would never be able to buy resources adequate to their needs as they defined them). They cannot take the stance that one of their major tasks is to refuse to assume exclusive responsibility for or to be seen as having the expertise to deal adequately with all the problems existing in schools. They cannot say aloud what they say privately: We will never have financial resources to cope effectively with our problems; unless we have call on community resources—unless we make the community share responsibility—the disparity between what we can do and what needs to be done will continue, and perhaps become greater [Sarason, 1976b, pp. 26–27].

The stance of the schools is typical of all agencies: Additional resources are needed, but it requires money to obtain them or to be the basis for an exchange of resources. As a consequence, agencies spend a good deal of time trying to get more money, in effect competing with each other for these additional financial resources. And that stance makes it inordinately difficult, and in practice almost impossible, to do three related things: to confront (if only as a possibility) that resources are and will be limited; to examine critically the accepted relationship between problems and solutions; and *to figure out possible ways in which agencies can learn to exchange resources in mutually beneficial ways and without finances being a prerequisite for discussion or the basis for exchange.* We have italicized the last point to emphasize the contrast between a typically "market" and "barter" way of viewing and exchanging resources. In the former, money is absolutely essential; in the latter, it is primarily a matter of determining whether there exists different needs that can be satisfied in mutually satisfying ways: "What do I have that somebody else can use in exchange for something of his that I need?" To be able to put the question in this way already suggests that vehicles need to be developed that not only maximize knowledge about available resources but also facilitate the processes of exchange. (As we shall see, networks can be such a vehicle.) The question is based on a way of thinking that is drastically different than that ordinarily governing relationships among agencies. In everyday practice, agencies do not seek each other out for the purposes of resource exchange; each agency sees itself as independent of all others, dependent only on its own subsidized resources to meet its goals, and energetically seeking new monies to purchase more resources. Each agency is an island, seeking ways to expand its land areas, fearing erosion from uncontrollable and unpredictable sources, and nurturing the fantasy that there must or there should exist the quantity and quality of resources that could ensure a safe and goal-fulfilling life.

Our experience led us to see how the usual way of thinking maintains or increases the gulf between what needs to be done and the resources available to do it. In suggesting that there may be other ways of thinking about the issue, we in no way are suggesting that the gulf can be eliminated, but rather that it can be reduced. If for no other reason than to reduce the size of the gulf, alternative ways of thinking have to be explored. Let us turn now to a consideration that stems in part from the universal complaint and that, in its own way, is no less universal.

The Sense of Community

The frequency with which the words *isolation, alienation, anomie,* and *loneliness* appear in conversation, social commentary, and literature is staggering. It is not appropriate here to discuss why this is the case, but it is appropriate to note that one of the contexts in which these feelings are experienced is the work setting. This is particularly true in human services settings where the perceived gulf between available resources and requests for service is large.[2] One of the consequences is that people within the agency

[2] In a recent book, *Work, Aging, and Social Change,* Sarason (1977) discusses and describes how work has become problematic in its satisfactions for professionals, especially those in human services settings. Of particular

feel they are unappreciated by the outside world, that is, they are an island of deprivation under the hostile watch of an armada intent on blockading the importation of new resources. This may seem like an extreme view, but in our experience, institutional or agency paranoia is the rule rather than the exception. It would be strange if it were otherwise, because each agency is in a basic sense directed to maintaining and increasing its resources to serve its constituents, and it expects all other agencies to adopt precisely the same position—which in fact they do. This is not only a barrier to true interagency exchange, but it often leads to the perception either that these agencies are in some ways in competition with each other, or that there is an obviously unfair distribution of resources among agencies. Far from an agency feeling itself to be part of a mutually supportive community of agencies—part of an "extended family," one of the bases for which is "I have call on you and you have call on me"—the agency as agency feels alone and beleaguered. What is insidious in this absence of the sense of community is that there is no viable way, no facilitating vehicle, whereby agencies can even know what the problems, dilemmas, and plans of other agencies might be. These internal issues are kept internal, only to surface when an agency seeks additional funds to increase its resources. The solution for these internal issues is almost never perceived in terms of possible interagency exchange, but prepotently in terms of new money to purchase new resources for the single agency. What deserves emphasis is that current practice not only minimizes exchange of information among agencies, and reduces almost to nil mutually beneficial exchange of resources, but also is an effective barrier to a sense of being part of a community of agencies. On the contrary, it reinforces and sustains the isolation of agencies from each other. And, finally, there is the frequent consequence that, within the single, isolated agency, its members begin to perceive each other in precisely the same way as we described agencies perceiving each

relevance is the chapter on professionals in community mental health centers, a relatively new type of helping agency in the history of which two major points are, unfortunately, quite clear: the failure to confront the fact of limited resources, and acceptance of the unrealistic perspective that resources available to these centers would increase.

other. That is to say, there is competition among members *within* an agency for its existing and new resources. So when we hear from an agency's members that there is a problem in communication, there is no true cooperation, and distrust rather than trust infuses working relationships, we are hearing within the agency what we hear among agencies. (It is no wonder that one of the fastest-growing industries in the past thirty years has been management consulting, whose task it is to alter the basis and quality of interrelationships in the work setting. And to the degree such consultants have met with success, it is largely due to having altered people's perception and knowledge of each other's problems, and to having created the conditions for noncompetitive mutually satisfying exchanges of information, plans, and resources.) The absence of a sense of community within and among agencies, accompanied as it so often is by a comparable absence of the sense of growth and accomplishment, leads to reduced motivation and cynicism. Just as the agency sees itself as an isolated island, so does the individual see himself within the agency. Few things are as destructive of an individual's morale as the recognition that one cannot accomplish one's goals in work, that one does not have the resources one needs, that one does not have access to knowledge and people who might be helpful, that one is not experiencing rejuvenation through new ideas and new relationships, that one is stagnating and alone with one's problems.[3] Again, it must be emphasized that what we are describing on the individual level is a mirror image of what is happening on the interagency level. Neither the agency nor the individual feels part of a network of relationships that maximizes mutual support and the exchange of resources—a type of network sustained not

---

[3] Guiding principles always bear the stamp of the interaction among man, moment, and locale. Our emphasis in this book on the interrelationships between limited resources and the psychological sense of community is but another instance of a more general social phenomenon: the realization that the divisions between work and nonwork, between reason and feeling, between science and philosophy, between abstractions about living and the concreteness of living itself, and between the values of individualism and the need for social rootedness have produced a chaos mirrored in people's feelings of impotence, drift, and isolation. The dream of progress through reason and

only because it increases resources available to people, or expands their knowledge, or provides new experience, but also because it dilutes the sense of loneliness.

The Goals of a Network

In describing the three considerations, we have tried to show their interrelations; that is, how, starting with the "myth of unlimited resources," we can better understand the origins of aspects of individual and agency behavior. Although these considerations are in no logical relationship to a concept of networks, it is instructive to note that in seeing the interrelations among these considerations we were in effect describing a type of network, one in which information and resource exchange, as well as personal and agency growth and development, encounter severe obstacles. It is a type of network in which planning and grappling with problems reflect the values of independence (personal or agency) and resource control, making it more likely that there will be competitiveness rather than cooperation among agencies. Agencies do see themselves as part of many networks—indeed, any human service agency could fill many pages listing and describing their formal and informal relationships with other agencies—and they pride themselves on

---

science has turned into an anxious nightmare or a pathetic but understandable flight from emptiness. No one in recent decades has illuminated our plight and its history better than Barrett (1962). His book deserves the closest study.

This is by way of indicating why in the chapters that follow we have given far more attention to a few guiding principles than to details of actions. We are not about to create a division between how to think and how to act, but because we are living in times when it is obvious that something is wrong with our basic categories of thinking, we have emphasized our thinking, although we by no means neglect how we acted in our efforts to be consistent with our principles. A network is an abstraction and since there are many types of networks there can be a problem in remembering them. The aim of this book is to deal as little as possible with abstractions, but rather to convey the concreteness of our experiences in trying to develop, what was for us, a different basis for interaction. As the reader will see in the review of the literature, the literature on network abounds in abstractions and is sparse in concreteness. It is also like so much of the scientific literature, relatively devoid of the "shoulds and oughts" of living. Obviously, we do not share this stance of neutrality. There is too much at stake.

their embeddedness in multiple networks as the hallmark of their responsiveness to community problems and their desire to cooperate. But the underlying governing "rules" for these network relationships are, first, that each agency can only depend on its own resources; second, that each agency has no "right" to call on the resources of another agency; and third, that it is the primary obligation of an agency to husband its resources to deal with problems as that agency defines them. In characterizing this type of network, we intend no criticism, and we are not asserting that it is without value. We do not doubt that many agencies see value in their network relationships and could give examples of productive mutuality among agencies. In our experience, however, this is uncommon. Far more common is a superficiality of relationships among agencies, tinged with competitiveness, standoffishness, and narrow self-interest and self-reliance.

Our aim has been not to criticize, but to understand the limitations of this type of network. And these limitations inhere not in personality or individual perversities or insensitivity to social issues, but rather in the failure to recognize the fact of limited resources and how this failure has the most serious consequences for the morale and efficacy of individual and agency functioning, as well, of course, of those who are clients. It is a failure, as one would expect, not peculiar to agencies, but to the nature of our society, in the sense that our history and culture have inculcated in all of us an unwarranted optimism about resources, an uncritical acceptance of growth and bigness, and an emphasis on the virtues of individualism that has obscured the hunger for community and mutuality in all areas of living.

As we reviewed and discussed how our past experience and present activities had drawn each of us to focus on a concept of networks, and how each helped round out the others' thinking, we came to see that we were in agreement about the considerations discussed earlier and that our task was to examine and describe what these considerations led to in action. It is one thing to become clear about the values, ideas, and goals of our type of network; it is quite another thing to act in ways appropriate to them. Agreement on values and goals is not always easy to obtain, but that is far less difficult than to sustain agreement in the course of action, which has a way of tearing apart the fabric of agreement and exposing the fragility of that fabric to the climate of action.

This book, then, attempts to answer several questions. How does one start a network that will reflect these considerations? What are some of the characteristics of the person or persons who start the network? How does one cope with the fact that this kind of network, based as it is on values and ideas rather different than those underlying other networks, requires changes in the way its participants ordinarily think and act? How do exchanges of resources come about without any financial exchanges? What kinds of financial or other material resources, if any, are required to initiate and sustain the network? How does one manage the growth of the network so that information and resource exchange are not adversely affected and a sense of belongingness and willing participation is maintained? What are the criteria by which one can judge network activities, and on what basis can one compare outcomes with those of other types of networks and interagency practices? As we shall see, many more questions will arise as we describe our experiences, not the least of which is how to describe our activities so that the reader does not miss the conceptual trees for the forest of description. Although the accuracy and completeness of description are of obvious importance, it is no more important (and at this stage of our knowledge and experience, it may be less important) than clarifying guiding principles that, when understood and used by others, may be more productively and illuminatingly applied than in our own efforts.

3

The Work
of Social Networks

ꝹꝹꝹꝹꝹꝹꝹꝹꝹꝹꝹꝹꝹꝹꝹꝹꝹ

We have seen that the word *network* has different meanings, and we have also briefly discussed a set of considerations giving direction to our effort to develop a network consistent with them. Before describing how that network was formed and developed, it might be helpful at this point to give examples of the kinds of activities engaged in by different members of the network. In giving these examples, we shall have little to say about rationale but rather more about the overt and sequential aspects of characteristic network activity. In a literal and deliberate sense, these are superficial descriptions, but they do provide for the reader a basis for conjuring up appropriate imagery about what people in the Essex network "do."

Environmental Education Project

1. *October 5, 1975.* In the process of talking with a friend, a network member learns that the county of which Essex is a part has

just received a Federal grant for developing environmental programs, including research in and improvement of water quality. The county has numerous lakes, streams, and reservoirs. The network member talks this over with another member, S. R., the network coordinator, who is coordinating environmental programs and who agrees to get more information about the law and the grant.[1]

2. *October 21.* S. R. meets with a representative of the task force with responsibility for the county program. The official explains different sections of the law, including the public participation requirements. S. R. tells her that a number of network members are quite interested and involved in environmental education, including one high school science teacher interested in placing students in real research situations. The official suggests a meeting between S. R. and the official charged with developing citizen participation.

3. *October 30.* The meeting takes place between S. R. and the "community participation specialist." The specialist explains that the law requires regular public meetings and asks S. R. to urge interested network members to attend the first meeting.

4. *November 5 and 20.* S. R. attends two public meetings together with A. A., who is a science teacher in the Essex high school. For the past year, A. A. has had several of his students doing research studies on the water quality of the local reservoir. Several years back an interstate highway was built adjacent to the reservoir, and there was concern about the effects of this construction and the traffic on water quality. The research suggested there was a basis for concern, and the teacher and his students have wanted the findings to be communicated to those who were in policy-making roles. It becomes clear at this meeting that the students' research is not likely to be given very much credence or attention. The two

---

[1] The need for and role of the network coordinator is taken up in a later chapter. Suffice it to say here that in the first year or so of the Essex network all coordinating functions were performed by Mrs. Dewar, about whom we will have much to say. The network then grew so quickly that it was impossible for her to continue giving the amount of time coordination required. The role of a network coordinator was then developed and a person (S. R.) chosen, who, under the tutelage of Mrs. Dewar, learned to share the coordinating function.

network members are quite vocal at these meetings. In fact, they request that the next meeting be held at the site of another network member (in the regional education services center) who is interested in more meaningful ties between county schools and county environmental programs.

5. *January 5, 1976.* S. R. meets with a faculty member from the local community college who was at the last public meeting, in order to discuss possible ways her students could get involved in network programs.

6. *January 14.* At this public meeting at the regional education services center, A. A. is elected to the policy board of the county water quality program. He begins to see that, in addition to research, there are other important ways in which one can make a difference, and other ways for his students to profit from participation in this program.

7. *January 22.* The county water quality program has a special task that needs to be done. S. R. takes the initiative and arranges a semester-long work-study program for a high school senior from a local school district. (This works out so well that S. R. was asked to make similar arrangements for 1976–1977.)

8. *January 28.* At this public meeting, A. A. and S. R. are elected to the citizen advisory council. Plans are discussed on how to bring together students and citizens on a more local basis, in order to focus more effectively on local concerns.

9. *February 11.* At this first local meeting (chaired by S. R.), there are a number of local citizens in addition to A. A. and his students. This is the beginning of a deliberate effort by A. A. to involve and expose students to the nature, purposes, opportunities, and dilemmas of citizen participation.

10. *April, May, June.* In each of these months, citizens and students hold local meetings. Four things characterize these meetings: articulate citizen discontent about their roles in existing practices and programs, discussion of professional research contracted for by citizen groups, how to involve more citizens, and how to become a force to be reckoned with. The proceedings of these meetings are always discussed by A. A. in his classes. Ways are sought whereby A. A. and his students could obtain, in conjunction with a somewhat distant but interested state university, more

sophisticated water-monitoring equipment in the hope of making the findings of the student research more credible to the policy makers.

11. *May 25.* A sophomore from one of the state universities, who is also an Essex resident, seeks to do an internship with the county water quality research program. This has come about because earlier that year S. R. has established contact through a mutual friend with a member of that university's environmental science faculty. S. R. had told this faculty member about the interest of the Essex network in environmental issues, and so, when he learned about the student's interests and residence, he had her arrange a meeting with S. R. The internship is satisfactorily arranged.

At the same time that the activities described were going on, other network members were involved with other individuals and agencies about environmental matters.

1. *November 1, 1975.* Three members of an independent graduate college of education who were part of the Essex network have described the network and its interests to a faculty colleague whose main interest was using the environment as a vehicle for integrative education for teachers and students. This colleague has called a network coordinator to request a meeting to discuss two items: his interest in and responsibility for the use of one section of a large state park for educational purposes, and the possibility that more of the county's school districts could become part of the effort.

2. *November 6.* A meeting is held. Attending are the faculty member, several network members, and a director of a local land conservancy center. The decision is made to contact the supervisor of regional educational services, B. B., to enlist his interest and support. A network member who serves on the board of that institution contacts him and arranges the meeting.

3. *December 12.* Attending the meeting are B. B., the regional supervisor, his chief aides in environmental studies, representatives of several school districts (one of them a network member), a representative of a federally supported national program in environmental education located in the county, a network coordinator, and the faculty member from the graduate college of education. The focus of the meeting is on the quality of facilities in the

particular section of the state park: its potential as an educational meeting and demonstration site. Everyone agrees that the site seems to present an unusual opportunity to meet multiple educational needs.

4. *January 21.* Three of the people from the December 12 meeting make a site visit to the section of the state park. The visit confirms the conclusion that the site has many possibilities and that as many school districts as possible should be drawn in.

5. *May 14.* The school district representative at the December 12 meeting, who is a network member, and a group of school principals from his district visit the site. The decision is made to involve a number of teachers in the program at the site for the coming summer. The program would be (among other things) under the leadership of the college faculty and would be available to teachers who already are involved in environmental approaches to education or to those who are not but wish to learn more about this approach in order to bring it meaningfully into their classrooms.

6. *June 3.* A group of teachers interested in the program visit the site.

7. *June 22.* Volunteer teachers (citizens with special interests and expertise) in the Essex elementary schools who teach conservation arrange a visit to the site.

8. *July.* Fourteen teachers begin the course at the site. They will receive graduate credit in the graduate college of education, with no payment of tuition.

We should remind the reader that this has been a skeleton, sequential description and was not intended to give the complex details characterizing many of the points in this sequence. Nor was it intended that the description would illuminate the rationale of the network. It was intended to give the reader some feel for what the network engaged in and the array of individuals and agencies who are brought in working contact with each other. Let us now turn to a very different type of "doing."

The University-High-School-Elementary School Project

1. *October 28, 1975.* In the hall of the Essex high school, three network members meet Mr. D., a social studies teacher who,

in the course of conversation, reports that he is interested in field placements for bright, highly motivated seniors. The network coordinator (S. R.) says he will get back to him in a few days.

2. *October 31.* S. R. and the teacher meet. The network is described and the teacher's needs explored.

3. *November 2.* S. R. speaks with his former faculty advisor at a large metropolitan university. In the course of the conversation, S. R. asks her what new research she is planning, and she briefly outlines her interests in the perception of children of "good news and bad news." Research has been done on adult perceptions and the question is to what extent and how children's perceptions differ. Some of her graduate students, as well as another colleague, are actively discussing possible research.

4. *November 5.* S. R. asks his former teacher if she would consider using the Essex schools for her project. The possibility of involving high school seniors in the conduct of the research is raised. She says she will discuss this with her graduate students.

5. *November 10.* S. R. speaks with the school district's supervisor of elementary education, who grants his approval but requests that S. R. also get the approval of the elementary school principals. S. R. asks another network member, a former chairperson of the School Board, to contact the principals.

6. *November 12.* The principals give their approval. S. R. speaks to the high school principal and gets his approval to seek ways of meaningfully involving selected seniors in the research.

7. *November 17.* S. R. speaks with the social studies teacher about possibilities for his students in the research project. The teacher takes the matter up with the principal, who agrees.

8. *December 1.* S. R., the social science teacher, and the university professor agree to a meeting at which the research project would be outlined from the point of view of the graduate school, the needs of each of the participating groups would be explored, and logistical problems confronted.

9. *December 8.* The meeting is held. Attending are the professor and a graduate student, the social studies teacher and six of his students, the high school principal and a representative of the superintendent of schools, and the network coordinator. Many problems and needs are discussed, but there is general agreement

that the needs of the seniors for an intellectually stimulating and technically enriching experience have to be met.

10. *December 17.* A "nuts and bolts" meeting between two graduate students, six high school seniors, and the social studies teacher. The substance of the research is discussed and the students make some helpful suggestions about substance and procedure that are accepted by the researchers. The students will collect all the data, and, with instruction from the graduate students, they will analyze the data (including content analysis).

11. *February 17–18, 1976.* The students run the study in one school after several weeks of working meetings with the graduate students.

12. *March 15.* A graduate student in the program and the seniors with whom she has worked complete another study in two other elementary schools, to meet her graduate program requirements.

13. *March 30.* The high school students present the project and describe their roles in it at a departmental colloquium at the university. They attend a course there in moral development and also begin didactic sessions on content analysis.

14. *April 13 to June 11.* The students work on data analysis.

15. *June 9.* The high school students, the social science teacher, and B. B. present the entire project at a meeting of the board of education, which urges that more of this activity should be encouraged.

16. *June 17.* At a general network meeting, a graduate student and the high school students present the history of the project and its personal and educational consequences for all of the participants.

More was going on in the Essex network than is suggested by our skeleton description. This does not mean that all that was going on had consequences as productive as those we have described in this chapter, or interconnected with as many individuals and agencies. There is, however, one characteristic that most of the network "doings" share: Their origins were unpredictable. For example, the university-high-school project started with a chance meeting in the halls of the high school; in the other project we described, the spark was a conversation between some network members and a colleague. One could say that these unpredictable, informal conversations or meetings generate possibilities someone in the network sees as consistent with its purposes. These possibilities become articulated opportunities, which, as often as not, take on a dynamic of their own. But to see, respond to, and seize these opportunities requires commitment to certain ideas, values, and strategies, that is, a way of perceiving and thinking that makes one vigilant to opportunities. It is not a set to see problems (to define situations in terms of deficits), but rather to see opportunities by which what different people have to offer is synergistically interconnected.

It is appropriate that we illustrate what we mean by "a way of perceiving and thinking that makes one vigilant to opportunities." One of the members of the Essex network accepted an important position in the most prestigious part of a public educational system in a somewhat distant state. We were, of course, happy for this person's new opportunity and sorry that she would be such a distance away. There was discussion about how she might continue as part of the network, recognizing the obstacles distance presented. Paraphrased, her response was as follows:

> There is no way that I will leave the network if for no other reason than that so many of you can be helpful to me where I am going, and I am assuming that I will be into things that will be of importance to you. But let me tell you how I have been thinking and what I have already done. For one thing, I made a list of all the people I personally know in that state and, to my amazement, I came up with a very long list on which are some people who are in other and less prestigious parts of the system of which I will be a part. And then I made another list of all the people and agencies who, as best I now can gather, would or could be affected by me in my position. The more I got into this, the more I realized that there were a lot of people and agencies who would feel hostile to and competitive with me, because they would perceive me either as possessing more resources than they or that I would be out to get more resources for what to them was an already favored and resource-loaded agency. So, my first task is, How do I get these

people to understand that I need them and they need me and a competitive struggle for resources would be stupid? How do I get them to see that under no circumstances will I duplicate what they have or, *noblesse oblige* style, make token gestures to sharing that leaves intact the weak–strong, inferior–superior, prestigious–nonprestigious type of relationship? And, finally, there is the task of putting these people and agencies in relationship to each other as in Essex, because I have every reason to believe that they view each other the way each of them is set to view me. What they don't know, but I do, is that I will not have the resources I need to do what I want, and that some of these people have what I need. I have learned a lot from being part of the Essex network, and, if I had to put it in a nutshell, it would be, If you go it alone, you will remain alone. As you well know, I am not a fan of the togetherness movement, but neither am I a fan of the heads-I-win, tails-you-lose philosophy. In coin tossing, one person wins and the other person loses, and I want no part of that.

Within months after she assumed her new position, she had begun an Essex-type network.

In the following chapters we shall describe the Essex network: how it developed, brought people together, and welded ideas of different people into a more coherent rationale for action.

4

The Emergence
of a Network

$\mathcal{N}$etworks exist; they are not created. In the course of a day, the networks to which one "belongs" may enlarge or contract (through death or estrangement) or remain apparently constant. We say "apparently," because, from a subjective standpoint, we may be completely unaware of any change in the extent and basis of our network relationships, and yet deliberate reflection or some special or unpredictable occurrence will often reveal that a quantitative and/or qualitative change has occurred. After all, we are not in the habit of reviewing our days in terms of whether or not our network relationships have been altered. This kind of review may be second nature to politicians and to others who by virtue of personality or work role see themselves in competitive situations requiring them to make frequent assessments of whom they know or should know. For most people, however, such a review only occasionally takes place. Novelists and

39

biographers, far more than social scientists, have illuminated the facts and role of networks in human affairs, that is, the far-flung web of relationships in which we are embedded and that we ordinarily do not acknowledge until changes internal or external to us force us to see and use that web.

The Essex network did not start at a particular point in time, but it existed as a possibility in the mind of Mrs. Dewar. What that sentence is intended to convey is that for a good part of her adult life this individual had become increasingly aware of and bothered by two characteristics of institutions (for example, hospitals, schools): the complaint that they lacked the resources to do what they should do, and their failure seriously to consider how they might gain more resources by developing ways whereby "outside people" normally unconnected with the agency would be given learning experiences productive to their own growth at the same time they were contributing to the setting. Put in another way, our communities contain many people eager to enlarge their knowledge, experience, sense of worth, and social contribution, but community agencies seem not to recognize their existence and potential contributions, and, furthermore, when their existence is recognized and utilized, it is on a "one-way street" basis. That is to say, the individual from the community is asked to volunteer time and energy to do something for the agency even though the performed task will minimally, or not at all, be experienced as growth producing. Explicitly, the satisfaction the individual should expect is in the sense of altruism, not in the quickening of the sense of learning. What Mrs. Dewar came to see was that agencies viewed community people (the "outsiders") not as potential learners and contributors but as objects of limited utility.[1] Agencies saw the world in terms of

[1] There is a more general point here that goes beyond the volunteer from the community, and that is that at all stages of education and life there are people who seek new experience and new directions and to whom our agencies and institutions are formidable barriers as sites for learning. Agencies generally are wary of requests from professionals who wish to use agency facilities for their own purposes, for example, to conduct some research. This wariness is understandable, but in our experience, these requests too often turn into "encounters," because neither the agency nor the professional approaches the other in a give-and-take manner. The agency is accustomed to "taking" from the ordinary volunteer and takes unjustified pride in having given the volunteer an opportunity "to give." But when the

their narrow definitions of needs and purposes, thereby shutting themselves off from potentially valuable resources. How, Mrs. Dewar asked, can one get agencies to view the community differently and to see the value of more *mutually* rewarding relationships? But this question went far beyond the relationships between agencies and individuals in the community. *The same question had to be asked about agency-agency relationships.* For example, how could hospitals and schools help serve each other's purposes and needs?

In effect, Mrs. Dewar was raising a most interesting and provocative question: Take any two individuals, or an individual and an agency, or two agencies (or any number of individuals and agencies in their different permutations and combinations)—to what extent can they match needs and purposes in mutually rewarding and productive ways? How can each gain from an exchange of resources? These were not idle questions to Mrs. Dewar, but stimuli to action. What the reader needs to know about her is that she is a "private," affluent citizen with a generalist background in service fields, very much involved in diverse community agencies and affairs, and perceived as a forceful, persistent, important, and knowledgeable individual. She was able to persuade leaders in several agencies to put her ideas into action, which they did with notable success. These were circumscribed efforts, in that they involved parts of complicated organizations, and they were successful in the following respects: They demonstrated that this form of "resource exchange" was possible; altered the thinking and lives of professional and lay participants, as well as of some skeptical administrators; and indicated that resource exchange did not necessarily require money exchange. There was one other "lesson" Mrs. Dewar learned from these experiences, and it was a consequence of the fact that all of the "matches" she was able to arrange between the agencies and individuals from the community almost always involved "helping" relationships. By focusing on what individuals could do or learn to do in a helping relationship—that is, by concentrating on and exploiting an individual's positive (healthy)

---

agency has to deal with requests from diverse professionals, it does not know how to transform the request so that both sides are giving and taking. But let us not scapegoat the agency. By and large, professionals are not noted for their stance of giving and taking.

rather than negative (unhealthy) characteristics, by building on assets rather than attacking deficits—everyone seemed to make enormous personal strides. Indeed, this simple but powerful lesson opened her eyes to the pervasiveness of the tendency of professionals to perceive people in terms of deficits.

This discussion is by way of indicating that, before the emergence of the Essex network, Mrs. Dewar already had developed for herself (and by herself) something akin to a concept of networks and how they could and should serve the needs of individuals and agencies. In one respect, her vision narrowed, in that she became interested in how schools and colleges could interact with community resource agencies for the purpose of enlarging the educational and vocational experiences of students and the educational opportunities for working members of institutions. In another respect, however, her vision or ambitiousness had considerably increased, in that there were few parts of the community she could not see as having a role to play. She knew the pieces; her task was to find out how they could be interconnected in a sustained way. In a literal sense, the question became: How does one increase the two-way flow between school and community?

If Mrs. Dewar was clear about her goals, as well as about the characteristics of the process by which they could be accomplished, she was less clear about where to start and with whom. In part, this lack of clarity reflected the overwhelming consequences of her sensitivity to the degree to which community resources were isolated from each other and the mammoth obstacles that presented to interconnectedness. What requires emphasis is that, although schools were in the center of her interest, they occupied this center as much for tactical reasons (that is, no one would deny the centrality of education to a community's responsibilities) as for the belief that the community contained resources that could dramatically enlarge students' knowledge of themselves, their community, and the larger society. As Mrs. Dewar said, "It really made no difference where you started. You could start any place in the community, but you had to connect that place with schools and on bases allowing everyone to feel they were getting something valuable out of the relationship." When one views the community in this way, the question of where to start and with whom is not easy to answer. Furthermore, Mrs. Dewar had no agency affiliation that could serve as a way to start the process of interconnectedness. She had status and perceived influence in the community, but these can be overrated as levers with which to move agencies in new directions.

Mrs. Dewar thought, why not examine the nearby community college as a nexus from which mutually beneficial interrelationships could be fostered? Why not make the community college a beginning base from which to develop an interagency network in relation to schools? Mrs. Dewar talked over these questions with Don Davies, who was then a visiting fellow at Yale's Institution for Social and Policy Studies (ISPS), and who had met her while he was Associate Commissioner of Education in the Office of Education in Washington. She chose Davies for two reasons. First, he had come to see that until the community was more meaningfully involved in educational decision making, one could not expect very much improvement in the quality of the educational experience. In fact, he gave up his post in Washington to come to Yale to think through and to develop what turned out to be the Institute for Responsive Education. What Davies stood for and wanted to accomplish was, so to speak, right up Mrs. Dewar's alley. The other reason for seeing him was to find out more about Yale's ISPS. What were its purposes? Would it be in its interests (practical or theoretical) to use Mrs. Dewar's community as a "laboratory"? Could this be done in a way that would be mutually rewarding both to ISPS and the community? Did ISPS have need for field placement of its students (graduate and undergraduate) and would these needs be met at the same time that these students were helping meet the educational needs of students in the public schools? Mrs. Dewar was not at all interested in having her community used as a laboratory animal. Just as she sought to bring about an alteration in the school's perception of and relationship to the community, she sought the same for community agencies in relation to schools. She was not asking something of the schools she was not asking of other settings.

Davies disagreed with Mrs. Dewar's aim to base her effort in any existing agency (for example, a community college, ISPS) and suggested that she develop an informal vehicle that could serve to link agency to agency, and agency to schools. He contended that, by being identified with one agency, it would unnecessarily increase the problem of forging interconnectedness of agencies. Davies also arranged a meeting between himself, Mrs. Dewar, and Seymour Sarason, who was also a member of ISPS. *This meeting had nothing to do with networks.* There were two items on the agenda for this meeting: What could Sarason tell Mrs. Dewar about the interests of ISPS faculty, and what were the thrusts of his research on work, aging, and education? To the first question, Sarason stated explicitly that it made no sense to talk of an *institutional* relationship between ISPS and Mrs. Dewar's community. ISPS was a collection of individuals who were interested in "real-life" problems, but it was a gross misperception of ISPS and Yale to think that any part of the university could or would enter into the kind of institutional affiliations Mrs. Dewar envisioned. What she might do, and Sarason was willing to help, was to meet those ISPS members whose research interests might indeed be furthered by having access to Essex as a laboratory. Sarason expressed the opinion that, among those who would be interested, very few would be willing to enter a relationship explicitly obligating them to meet some need in the Essex community. To the second question, Sarason explained how he had become interested in a developmental conception of aging and how the dynamic interrelationships between education and work influenced the psychological sense of aging. What school children learned about the world of work, and the characteristics of the process by which they considered and chose career paths, too frequently led to dissatisfaction with work and self. Sarason could not agree more with Mrs. Dewar that the isolation of schools from the community—the idea that education should take place primarily within the walls of schools—was a disastrously narrow view of the nature of the educational process. Yes, Sarason was willing to talk further with her about a relationship involving him, his students, and the Essex schools.

The Significance of the First Meeting

It is relatively easy to describe what people say at a meeting. It is far more difficult, obviously, to describe what they felt, that is, that large part of the experience for which the spoken words are at best inadequate, and at worst misleading symbols. The chemistry of meetings, like the chemistry of matter, is ordinarily not visible. We could have described that first meeting in great detail in the sense of "He said this and she said that" and misled the reader in believing that he understood what went on and what was accomplished. From the standpoint of what developed over the next few years, that first meeting had several significances.

First, each of the three people had a personal, self-serving agenda. And by self-serving, we do not intend a pejorative connotation. At the same time, however, each person was by virtue of ideology and temperament predisposed to narrow somewhat the scope of self-interest in order to accommodate to the interests of others. In terms of background and experiences, these were three rather different people, and yet, despite this diversity, they recognized that in terms of conceptions, values, and interest there was surprising overlap.

Second, for several years before this meeting, Sarason had been trying conceptually to deal with the interrelationships among three issues: (1) the fact that resources are always limited; (2) the sense of constriction and isolation that many people experienced in their work and personal lives; and (3) the inadequacies of theories of action (as well as the failure of social activists) to confront directly the problems of resources, isolation, and work dissatisfaction. This explains why he had a cordial relationship with Davies, who, in somewhat more restricted ways, was dealing with the same issues in regard to community participation in educational decision making. It also helps explain why throughout that meeting Sarason became increasingly intrigued with what Mrs. Dewar seemed to be groping for. We say "seemed" because little in what she said led directly to Sarason's central concerns, and, it will be recalled, most of that conversation was about education in relation to work, career planning, and lifelong learning—as well as the nature and thrust of Yale's ISPS. And yet, Sarason sensed that what she was after related to all of his central concerns.

Third, the word or a concept of *network* never came up in that meeting. But that was precisely the concept that Sarason was developing to bring his central concerns into some conceptual relationship to each other as a guide to action for change. Why, he had been asking himself, did so many strategies for change misfire or bring about counterproductive results? The more he examined instances of failure, the more clearly he saw how almost completely they had ignored the presence, strength, and diversity of the networks to which the individuals, groups, and agencies who were the objects of change or help belonged. Ignoring these facts of social and institutional life not only guaranteed resistance and opposition to change, but also increased polarization that had adverse personal effects on everyone. Far from leading to a sense of community and personal growth, a frequent consequence was the sense of divisiveness, isolation, and disillusionment. Finally, these failures had one glaring feature in common: to bring about change required additional resources that could not be obtained without new monies (usually a good deal of them), a stance that effectively bypassed the question, How can we locate the resources we need, wherever they might be in the community, and arrange for their exchange (barter fashion) in ways perceived as mutually rewarding? At that very first meeting, Sarason sensed that Mrs. Dewar, albeit less clearly than he, was or would be dealing with these issues. As he later put it, "In the realm of human resources, she was the best matchmaker I had ever seen. And she did not charge for her services."

Fourth, money was never discussed at that meeting. Indeed, what was remarkable was the unverbalized agreement that, if we were to develop a working relationship, it would be because each of us had something to give and get from each other. Mrs. Dewar wanted resources for her community, Davies was interested in community participation in educational decision making, and Sarason and his students would be in on the ground floor as participants and documenters of another action project.

The first meeting was more than pleasant. Nothing was "accomplished," nobody promised anybody anything, and, although all persons said they would be willing to meet again, this was less because anyone felt strongly that "something would happen" and more because we had found the first meeting interesting. (As we shall see in Chapter Five, the substance and quality of network meetings and the balancing of different perceptions are absolutely crucial in understanding the waxing and waning of the quality of *any* network's activity.)

This characterization of the first meeting is incorrect in one respect. Specifically, Sarason (not Davies) misperceived Mrs. Dewar's propensity for action. To her, Davies and Sarason were resources to be garnered for her purposes and the quicker she exposed them to the possibilities in her community, the quicker would a mutually rewarding relationship be established.

The Network Emerges

Within a few weeks of the initial meeting, Mrs. Dewar arranged a series of meetings for Davies and Sarason with small community groups. Representatives from business, schools, hospitals, public officialdom, and social agencies came to these meetings. It obviously says a good deal about Mrs. Dewar's knowledge of and status in the community that she could arrange such meetings. These were not easy meetings. Mrs. Dewar would ask Davies and Sarason to talk about their interests in the context of their willingness to pursue these interests in ways that might be helpful to relevant parts of the community. Then the community representatives would be asked to respond. Several things seemed apparent in these meetings. First, Davies and Sarason had established their credentials with Mrs. Dewar, but there was no way they could do the same with the community representatives at these meetings. Second, we were "outsiders" from a prestigious university and it was unclear to them what our "real" agenda was. Third, Mrs. Dewar was not sensitive to how unfamiliar the concept of "bartering for resources" is to agencies or their representatives. Davies and Sarason felt pulled along by Mrs. Dewar's persuasiveness, energy, and good intentions, but uncomfortable with the feeling that nothing would develop. This was unfortunate, because some of the people at these meetings had articulated to Mrs. Dewar their feelings of isolation and their need for some kind of university resource, a need to have ready access to what was going on in their fields in other parts of the country and world, as well as a need to learn better how to interact with their own community. They were totally unclear about what mechanism or system might achieve this. Some were enthusiastic and eager to tie in with Yale, thinking mostly in terms of available consultants. There were others, of course, who feared the social scientists' history of using institutions strictly for their own purposes. These meetings had some of the elements of "show and tell," elements not conducive to initiating give-and-take dynamics. These were uninteresting meetings, in the sense that people of somewhat similar views and interests were not sitting around and playing with ideas and possibilities, searching for ways that would justify remaining together over time, and leaving the meeting with the feeling that, however small the change, the world did look different.

There was one major consequence to these meetings. In the process of participating in and then discussing each meeting, we had become a network. That is to say, we were in frequent contact with each other (Mrs. Dewar saw to that!), considering opportunities, clarifying our goals and concepts, and increasingly becoming, to some extent, part of what the others were into. Without, so to speak, taking a vote or even noting it, we had decided to stick together, to be on call to each other. One other consequence of these meetings was that Davies and Sarason became familiar with Mrs. Dewar's community as well as with a few individuals who, much later on in the history of the network, truly became related to it.

The Problem of Description

It is literally impossible to paint a tree in all of its nuances and complexity. It cannot be done by any artist, however talented. A tree consists of too many leaves, branches, and shadings to be reproduced. But the artist does not intend a realistic reproduction, and the viewer of his artistic effort does not demand it. We are faced with a similar task in describing a network, and in some ways a more difficult task, because at any one point in time a network consists of many individuals in actual and potential relationships to each other. And the relationships between one individual and others in the network can vary as a function of scores of factors. For example, Sarason's relationship to Mrs. Dewar was not the same as it was with Davies, and Davies' relationship to Mrs. Dewar was different than it was with Sarason. One of the early additions to the network was N. Dickon Reppucci, a colleague of Sarason's. His relationship to Mrs. Dewar and Davies was obviously qualitatively different than it was to Sarason. Furthermore, each member of a network differs considerably in the number and kinds of networks of which the person or others may consider himself/herself a member, and, crucially, by virtue of differences in such variables as age, status, experience, and personality, members of a network can vary considerably in the quantity and quality of resources they can offer either as individuals or as seekers of resources from other networks. What we are suggesting here is that, in the early days of the Essex network, consisting as it did of no more than a handful of individuals in actual interrelationships, it would be an overwhelming task to describe these interrelationships. If, in addition, we assumed the task, as we did from time to time, of listing and describing our relationships with people who potentially could or should become part of our network, the task became truly overwhelming, at the same time that it confirmed us in the belief that the resources potentially available were enormous.

The difficulty of description is exponentially increased by another characteristic of networks: They change over time, very brief periods depending on new problems and opportunities. We shall have more to say about this in a later chapter. Suffice it to say here that the kind of network we are describing is a loose, informal, voluntary "arrangement" of individuals, each of whom has call on the others, at the same time he or she is untrammeled in their activities. The network has no formal decision-making processes. One of its major purposes is catalytic and matchmaking in nature. *In this kind of network, what will come up or happen in between network meetings is unpredictable.*

In certain fields or from particular theoretical perspectives, it is important to be able to describe and quantify networks in terms of how they grow or decline in size, and how these processes reflect changes external to the network. From our perspective, these are not unimportant questions, but they are secondary to describing the conceptual and philosophical considerations that led to the Essex network, and to the kinds of "glue" that kept it together and the conceptual development to which activities gave rise. We did not enter into the network with the primary aim of some day judging our efforts by how many people we had brought into new relationships to each other, although that would not be irrelevant to our purposes. Nor did we enter the network because we were in agreement about specific kinds of changes we wanted to effect in certain settings, although such changes also would not be irrelevant to a future evaluation. The truth is that it took several months for us to clarify why we were sticking together and what we hoped to accomplish. What got clarified were certain values and ideas that had general applicability and about which we were in complete agreement.

First, redefining resources in terms of a mutually rewarding form of barter exchange that also stimulated further exchanges and would significantly increase the capacity of individuals and agencies to achieve their goals. The barter type of resource exchange is no panacea, but it held promise of significantly increasing the extent and efficiency of the use of resources.

Second, one of the major consequences of redefining resources in this way is that it enlarges one's sense of capability and worth, increases one's knowledge of and experience with other people and settings, and enables one to begin to break out from the parochialism of one's work setting. The efficacy of one's own work becomes enhanced, providing satisfaction with one's own job and a sense of contributing to that same feeling in others. With this comes the feeling of trust and reliance that others will pull their weight, that responsibility does not rest solely on one's own shoulders—in short, that one is not alone. Diversity, both intellectual and social, can come into one's life. One's sense of community quickens because one is engaged in "give and get" relationships with more and diverse people.

Third, what is true for the individual is no less true for the abstraction we call an *agency,* or *setting,* or *institution.* Walled in by tradition, professional preciousness, and the need to protect and increase resources under its control, the agency cuts itself off from commerce with its surround, the kind of commerce that exploits the agency's protean possibilities for service and change.

Fourth, education is a lifelong need and process. It is not a "thing" that begins in kindergarten and ends with graduation from high school or college. What students learn in school about themselves and society is distorted, in large part because they and their teachers are separated from the larger society. In the most unwitting and yet powerful ways, students accept the attitude that education is a time-limited affair, a retreat from the world at the same time it is a preparation for later coping with that world. In recent years, and at all levels and in all segments of education, there has been recognition that this attitude has become counterproductive, and there is greater willingness to consider how to lower the barriers between students and school personnel, on the one hand, and "outside" adults and community settings, on the other hand. What has received less discussion is how this can be achieved to begin to meet not only the needs of students, but also the needs of these adult "outsiders," for intellectual stimulation, new work roles, and new relationships. To see education as a process exclusively for young people, to see schools as places to which the "outsiders" give something to the young, is to ignore the fact that these "outsiders" have educational desires no less than do the young.

Fifth, ours was a network for action, but it was not tied to a particular type of setting. By the very nature of our ideas and values, we were a resource-locating and resource-matching vehicle in a complex community, and the purposes of matching were twofold: to alter people's conceptions about resources, work roles, and relationships; and to reduce people's feelings of isolation, frustration, and routine. It made no difference where and with whom we started, because our actions would always be guided by the question: How do we bring people together so that by exchanging, they are generating new energies, possibilities, and capabilities?

These agreements sound virtuous and ambitious, if not presumptuous. The fact is that we were only minimally concerned with the extent of impact, if only because in those early days we were so few in number, uncertain about tactics, and quite sensitive to the fact that between agreements and action is an obstacle course few agreements can successfully traverse. *What these agreements truly reflected was our evaluation of how each of us in those early days had benefited from our meetings in terms of new knowledge, new possibilities for experience, and the sense of belonging to "something" we wished (needed) to sustain.* We had demonstrated to our satisfaction (without ever saying it) that our ideas and values were working for us. In seeking to enlarge the network, could we continue to be consistent to these ideas and values? What problems would we encounter? In what ways were we atypical and, therefore, without sound basis for making generalizations? If asked to do so, how would we describe what we were doing, how we were doing it and why?

We have answered the last question, at least in relation to the early days of the Essex network. If it had been possible to give only a half-complete description of what we did, the reader would have found himself lost in a forest of names, places, meetings, agendas, phone calls, and so on. We would have been describing facts at the expense of truth: We enjoyed each other, we were learning from each other, we were gaining clarity about what we wanted to accomplish, we were willing prisoners of certain ideas and possibilities, and we wanted to stay together.[2] Indeed, if we attempted a comprehensive description, every reader would have been asking this question: How did we stay together that first year, in light of the fact that we were unsuccessful in several efforts to enlarge the network by interconnecting it with community settings? One reason for continuing was that at least one important member of the community (a member of the school board) became part of the actual network, and several faculty members from a well-known, innovative graduate college of education became interested in what we were trying to do and asked to be involved if and when we thought they could play a role. Without question, however, the major reason was Mrs. Dewar's enthusiasm, persistence, and constant scanning for ways to test our ideas, that is, to go beyond discussing and clarifying.

So we are back to where we began this chapter: Mrs. Dewar. There is no doubt that the links in the strength of the emerging network would have been much diluted that first year if she did not have the time to give to it, or the passionate commitment to the ideas and values that were giving order and stimulation to our lives and relationships, or her strong need to serve her com-

---

[2] In this narrative we run the risk of creating the impression that we were a self-appointed rescue squad throwing out lifelines to drowning people. We are deceiving neither ourselves nor the reader when we assert that our perception of ourselves was not that naive or presumptuous. And yet it was the case that many people who joined the network explicitly verbalized that we had introduced something necessary and positive in their lives.

munity. One other unusual factor needs to be noted: She tended to view Sarason as crucial to what was emerging, and Sarason viewed her similarly. It was obvious that Sarason respected, admired, and liked her. This was no "Herr Professor–Ms. Laywoman" relationship. It would be unfair and incorrect to say that she was the activist and Sarason the conceptualizer, because she has wrestled seriously with conceptualizations of what she had experienced and Sarason was disposed to act as a way of learning (Sarason, 1974). And yet Mrs. Dewar was the network leader in the sense that she took and kept the initiative, and if she had not done so in that year, the story would be quite different. We shall return to the role and issues of leadership in human networks in a later chapter. Let us turn now to a meeting that was the turning point in the growth and character of the Essex network.

The Beginning of Action

Mrs. Dewar had long been intrigued with the different ways by which the needs and desires of college and high school students for field experiences could be matched to the enrichment of the educational vocation of both groups. She knew that teaching personnel in both settings were always seeking field placements that could be adequately supervised and could truly be justified by educational-intellectual-vocational criteria. Not surprisingly, she was knowledgeable about studies (for example, Gartner, Kohler, and Riessman, 1971) of "children teaching children" and had for years exchanged ideas with the authors who illustrated her belief in the potentials of resource exchange in the context of a helping relationship. In fact, she believed that the prepotent response of schools (elementary, high school, college) to seek to purchase special resources for special problems obscured their recognition of what they could do by redefining existing resources. This interest returned to the fore as Mrs. Dewar learned more about a new state liberal arts college very near her community. Why not try to put together the needs of this college and those of several other institutions with those of the school system? Through a series of small, exploratory meetings, she was able to arrange for a larger meeting hosted by the new liberal arts college. The following people were invited and attended:

1. Mrs. Dewar.
2. The dean of social sciences of the new liberal arts college.
3. Sarason and two of his students.
4. Mrs. H., who had been on the local and county boards of education and was serving on the board of various other agencies.
5. Mr. L., who was chairman of the department of human services of the community college.
6. Mr. T., principal of the local high school.
7. Ms. U., the director of a moderately large, residential educational institution for disadvantaged, high-risk children from a nearby large metropolitan area. Ms. U was black, forceful, articulate, and always in search of ways to help her children and staff.

This meeting differed from all previous "large" ones in several instructive respects. The stated agenda was circumscribed and everyone who attended had a professional stake in the topic. In previous meetings, the agenda had for the participants some of the characteristics of an inkblot. The meeting was not for the purpose of putting the Yale contingent on display, although their presence obviously would require explanation.[3] Finally, in contrast to previous meetings, a major purpose, aside from discussing the agenda, was to provide an opportunity for the community people to get to know each other. We could assume they would perceive what they had in common, and we knew that some

---

[3] In the preparatory meetings, Mrs. Dewar had briefed people well on what she hoped would come out of a larger meeting, and she also explained in concrete fashion what the Yale group's interests were and what their involvement might be. Those who came to this meeting were told, at the very least, that it had "intentionality," that is, it could be the basis for cooperative action. But one should never assume that what people have been told, they understand or agree with in ways one intended. So, although the groundwork for a potentially productive meeting had been laid, we did not assume that everyone was starting from the same kind of understanding or degree of commitment.

were familiar to each other, but we also could assume they had never had the opportunity to discuss communalities in their roles and needs. In short, the meeting had the characteristics of specificity of task and homogeneity of participants.

Mrs. Dewar chaired the meeting, although, as it turned out, it was more of a moderator role, because the participants were very articulate people, not only quite eager to talk about what they were doing and up against, but also to respond to what others were saying. Three things happened at the meeting that give something of its flavor. At one point, Mr. L. from the community college offered to share his field service resources with the others on some mutually satisfying basis. The second instance emerged from a discussion of the shortage of day-care facilities where graduates from the Human Services Department of the community college could find employment, a discussion that seemed somewhat removed from the agenda until Mrs. Dewar pointed out that there were (and would increasingly be) unused classrooms in the elementary schools and asked why could these not be used for day care in ways that would give roles and experiences to college students and public school students? (This intrigued everyone.) The third instance was a fascinating interchange brought on by Ms. U.'s light, direct, but tactful criticism of the college representatives because they seemed to have no interest in one of her major problems: providing educational programs for her staff in ways and at sites convenient for them. She pointed out that her institution was used by agencies (including the community college) for *their* educational and training needs, but asked what could they do for her staff. She made it clear that she was interested in exchanging and not giving resources. But she agreed that her school could become the network's first communal work-study setting.

This meeting was like the first one we described: It was intellectually and interpersonally *interesting,* as well as producing agreements, so that there was never any question of *whether* there would be a next meeting, but *where.* It was natural that it should be convened as soon as possible at the site of the future field placements, Ms. U's institution. But there was one other feature of that meeting that came to characterize network meetings and in part explains why people, in increasing numbers, came regularly—that feature was unpredictability about what would come up in discussion and what possibilities would emerge. This is not to suggest that people came either because of the unpredictability factor or the stimulating character of meetings. These were important variables, but they would not have been sufficient if the participants did not see movement to the satisfaction of the needs of their work setting.

So it was interesting and people agreed to meet again, but a hard-nosed critic would ask: So what? What happened that any member could not have achieved on his own? This is a deceptively clear question. Let us rephrase the question this way: What aspects of the rationale for the network were either fulfilled or set in motion? When put in this way, a three-part answer can be found. First, the meeting seemed to spark some sense of common purpose, some fleeting sense of community. *We would argue that without creating this climate no other aspect of the network's purposes had the possibility of fulfillment.* In contrast to all previous meetings (except the first between Dewar, Davies, and Sarason), this one took on the kind of ambience for which we had been hoping. This is not to say that everyone at the meeting showed a clear willingness to "give or get," or that the meeting had the characteristics of a love fest. Rather it is to say that by the end of a three-and-a-half-hour meeting a lot of busy people felt something was materializing and were eager to be with each other again. Second, at no point in discussion of ideas, possibilities, and problems did anyone bring up finances as an obstacle to the exchange of resources. No one questioned Mrs. Dewar's and Sarason's remarks about the kinds of exchanges we thought necessary and desirable. Finally, during the years of the network, every individual at that meeting was active in network activities and helped achieve its growth and purposes. In the next chapter, we take up the bedeviling task of describing that growth.

5

Significant Meetings and Network Growth

The meeting we described at the end of the previous chapter was obviously written from the combined perceptions of Dewar and Sarason.[1] In truth, we cannot assert that we know what the other participants "really" felt about the meeting, although when it was over, most of them expressed satisfaction with it. About one of the participants, Sarason and Dewar differed in their view of his motives and intentions, that is, of all the participants he seemed to express skepticism as to what we were about, and he seemed, on an overt level, the most concerned about what he could get out of the group. Mrs. Dewar had no cause to question his stance, but Sarason felt strongly that this participant

[1] Don Davies had left Yale to take up a position in Boston University. Although he was still part of the network, it was more a potential than an actual part. Mrs. Dewar was in frequent touch with him, Sarason less so, because of their interest in his Institute for Responsive Education. To date, he never attended another network meeting, but at different times he has provided information useful to us and other members of the network.

was too concerned with self-interest to stay long in a "give-and-get" network. We mention this difference in perception because it is so easy for people like Dewar and Sarason to be unaware that their perceptions are inevitably colored by many factors, not the least of which are personality and personal investment. Mrs. Dewar, more than Sarason, tended then and later to underestimate obstacles and overestimate commitment. On the other hand, Sarason tended to obsess about the world of obstacles and to underestimate the level of people's commitment. But differences in perception between the two could also be assumed to be operating among the other participants at the meeting. We are, of course, suggesting that describing *a* meeting raises all the age-old problems of the differences among perceptions, facts, and the truth. These are not abstract problems or a ritualistic recognition of or obeisance to the requirements of science or objectivity. After all, we are attempting description in the hope it will be helpful to others, and to the extent that our descriptions unreflectively confuse what we think we perceived with what others perceived and experienced, we are misleading the reader. It is awareness of this that required us to give attention to the consequences of meetings, and in the case of the last meeting, we reported the fact that, with one exception, all the participants remained active in the network.[2] But that fact hides a truth: Not all of the network activities of these participants fulfilled *all* of the goals of the network's purposes. If any goal was truly achieved, it was the sense of community. In terms of resource exchange, however, this was less true, although that judgment raises questions we shall try to illuminate by discussing the immediate consequences of that meeting.

The Immediate Consequences of the Meeting

One of the initial consequences of the meeting was that students from the liberal arts and community colleges were placed

[2] An example of the problem of description. This narrative was written in the summer after the third year of the network's existence. The sentence about the "one exception" is true in that up until the end of the third year that individual could not be considered a member. But toward the end of that third year, some opportunities developed that brought that person actively back into the network's activities in ways consistent with the network's rationale.

in work-study arrangements and supervised internships at Ms. U.'s residential center. These arrangements were obviously important to the colleges and their students; but what was the residential center getting in exchange? One could argue that the center was getting some additional manpower, because the college students did perform certain tasks, and it also could be argued that the center staff supervising them were being intellectually stimulated, as is almost inevitably the case when one is contributing to the development of young prospective professionals. These are legitimate arguments, but they overlook the fact that at the top of Ms. U.'s priority list was obtaining advanced education and training for *her* staff. If Ms. U. willingly entered these arrangements, it was with the hope that over time the nature of the resource exchange would be more weighted in her favor. A second consequence of that meeting stemmed from the fact that almost all the children in the residential center were black and a portion of them attended the local suburban high school, most of whose students were white. There were the usual problems, albeit on a much smaller scale than one might have expected, due in large part to Ms. U. (also black), whose ability to diagnose and manage difficult situations was nearly unrivaled. Would the Yale contingent be interested from a research standpoint in evaluating aspects of the center's internal activities in terms of school and community relationships? The answer, of course, was in the affirmative, and it took a couple of months to work out the necessary arrangements. N. Dickon Reppucci, a colleague of Sarason's at Yale, was eager to join the network because of the training opportunities it might afford his students, in addition to the fact that his research interests centered around the nature, structure, and problems of child-serving institutions. That study went on over a year and, although it encountered obstacles and its focus had to be changed somewhat, it culminated in a written evaluation of her setting for Ms. U. From the Yale perspective, this was a magnificent learning experience, and Ms. U. thoroughly enjoyed her teaching and personal relationships with the Yale students (although she understandably complained from time to time about how much of her time was going to the project and the Yale students). Again, however, one has to ask if Yale's benefits were not discernibly greater than those accruing to Ms. U. and her center. Let us postpone answering this question until one other consequence of the meeting is noted. It will be recalled that members of a prestigious graduate college of education wished to be part of the network, but their distance from Mrs. Dewar's community was a real obstacle. When she informed them by telephone (she kept actual and potential network members informed!) about what happened at the meeting, it led to a relationship between this college and Ms. U. The first tangible result was a meeting at the center, to which came black and Puerto Rican master's degree students planning careers working with inner-city children in residential settings. This was a one-day meeting that was mutually rewarding to everyone. And what did Ms. U. or her center gain from arranging and hosting the meeting? Note that the form of this question distinguishes between Ms. U. and her center, because what an individual gets out of network participation should not be confused with what his or her agency gets. In Ms. U.'s case, three factors help explain her willingness for her center to be "exploited." First, she had very definite positions about society's obligations to children in general, and neglected, underprivileged children in particular. Second, she felt it to be her obligation to educate white society about the black experience, especially well-intentioned whites who did not recognize the degree to which they were imprisoned by stereotypical attitudes and concepts. Third, Ms. U. enjoyed the give and take of debate (she rarely lost). What we are suggesting is that, as an individual, Ms. U. was gaining as much as she was giving. She *knew* she was influencing people, and she *knew* she was gaining friends.

If we distinguish between individual and agency benefits, it is not for the purpose of downgrading, for purposes of evaluation, the nature of the resource exchange between agencies, but rather to emphasize an easily overlooked point: *We are describing a network of individuals in relationship to each other, and to the degree that individual needs are satisfied, particularly in the earliest phases of network formation, it establishes the precondition for an equitable barter exchange among agencies.* We participate in a network as individuals, not as officially designated representatives of agencies. It is as agency representatives that we seek resources for our agencies, but it is as individuals that we decide how seriously we should attempt to match network resources to agency needs. And in making that choice, our own personal, intellectual, and social needs are probably decisive. Evaluation of the nature of network resource exchange must distinguish, to some degree at least, between the gains to individuals and agencies. The fact is that the meeting did result in mutually satisfying (albeit unequal) resource exchange among agencies, and this happened with a speed explainable in large measure by the preparation for and the ambience of that meeting. Our description of the consequences of the meeting is incomplete, if not misleading, in that it neglected a process or series of minimeetings (over the phone or in person) that was less a "consequence" than a process characteristic of and natural to the Dewar-Sarason relationship.

Between-Meeting Meetings

Following the meeting whose consequences we have been describing, as well as all subsequent meetings, Dewar and Sarason would hold frequent discussions around three questions: What went on, overtly or covertly, at the meeting? What possibilities were raised by the meeting? How do we transform these possibilities into actions or relationships consistent with the purposes of the network? What these questions signified was that Dewar and Sarason felt *responsible* for the network, not in the sense that it was *their* network, but in the sense that by helping to form the network they had taken on the obligation to make it work, an obligation no one else at that point could be expected to take on. This meant that, in the most self-conscious way, the two of them had to attend to as many aspects of the activities as possible, be sensitive to opportunities, and work at making these opportunities realities. Mrs. Dewar, far more than Sarason, would come away from a meeting with what (to Sarason) was an overwhelming array of interconnections that might be forged either by virtue of the people at the meeting or the ideas that had been expressed. This way of perceiving and thinking had become second nature to Mrs. Dewar, and it led to the distinction between actual and potential network members; that is, potential members were those who could or should become active when we would have more time (or there would be a more appropriate occasion) to seek their effective participation. Sarason was less enamored with the quantity of interconnections and he positively feared quick growth because his experience had led him to conclude that quick growth, more than any other factor, killed good ideas and new settings. To exult over quick growth at the same time that such growth is leading to inconsistency between values and actions is to be victimized by a production ethic.[3] How and at what pace to grow were questions we tried never to lose sight of and, as we shall see in a later chapter, these questions ultimately required a different answer than the one we gave in the early phases when Mrs. Dewar could keep in touch with everyone and everything going on. The point to be stressed is that, from the time a meeting ended to the beginning of the next one, Mrs. Dewar and Sarason were in frequent contact with each other, agonizing over what happened and should happen, over substance and process. We say *agonizing* because to an outside observer that might seem an appropriate adjective. To both of them, these were instructive and exciting learning experiences.

Aside from reviewing the previous meeting, these "meetings between meetings" concerned when and how to follow up on agreements made between two or more people to meet to discuss further an idea or proposed cooperative action. Generally speaking, Mrs. Dewar would wait a week or two before inquiring whether the meeting had taken place or a date for it had been set. Early on we learned that when, during a meeting, two or more people agreed to

---

[3] Mrs. Dewar in no way accepted sheer growth as a criterion of progress. Her tendency to see interconnections to be exploited was a direct reflection of her goal to enlarge and sensitize people's knowledge and use of the potentials in their *total* environment. In a letter to Sarason, she put it this way: "I think we must distinguish between growth that is proliferation with nothing new added, and growth that adds missing elements and new dimensions that constitute quality, that is, where, in fact, quantity *is* quality. Without certain categories of organizations available to individuals and institutions, we don't have the organizational gamut that reflects the true potential of an environment. Without a gamut of disciplines, we lack the conceptual elements available in our culture, which also should be part of the individual and institutional environment. The components of our action and study program must represent the total environment." This explanation of when "quantity becomes quality" indicates why her conception of the phrase "total environment" is not a cliché or empty rhetoric. For her, the total environment is something to be mapped, understood, and exploited for one's own growth (not aggrandizement). And by virtue of the fact that each of us is part of that total environment we have to be prepared to be "exploited."

meet some time after it (for example, "we will be in touch with each other"), they usually were underestimating how the nature of their very busy lives would conspire against follow-through action. What people agree to during a meeting in the flush of enthusiasm and excitement has a way of looking different when they return to the demands and routine of their working lives. Mrs. Dewar's task was gently and diplomatically to inquire about whether the agreed-on meeting had or would take place. She also had to prod without being too intrusive. But she found eager acceptance of this "expediter" role, sometimes solving the status bind that stops communication: "I left word, and she hasn't returned my call." This is a particularly sensitive set of problems in the early phases when people still find network meetings somewhat strange; they are uncertain about what the network leader is "really up to," and their sense of comfort with each other is by no means well established. The task for Mrs. Dewar was made both harder and easier by the fact that she was not a professional, had no agency affiliation, obviously was not in need of material resources from anyone, and was passionately devoted to certain ideas not always articulated well by her. (This may be unfair to her, because if some people did not quickly comprehend what she was saying, it was in part because what she was saying was literally new to or in conflict with customary thought and practice.) Professionals and their agencies are not used to dealing with a Mrs. Dewar.

Relationships among network members cannot be left to chance, especially in the early phases of the network. They have to be forged, and that was Mrs. Dewar's task. More important than enlarging the network or even plunging into actions and programs was strengthening members' knowledge of, respect for, and comfort with each other. "Real life," however, rarely is structured to allow one to adhere to one's priorities, and we found ourselves doing something about everything. For example, concerns about day-care facilities (their numbers, quality, and myriad uses) were an important part of the discussion in the meeting we have been describing. In one of the "meetings between meetings," Mrs. Dewar pointed out that the county was receiving federal funds to hire and retrain unemployed people and that the county's director of manpower, who would be responsible for the program, probably had not had time to think through how these programs could be max-

imally productive. Maybe he would be interested in meeting us
(Dewar and Sarason) to see if there was a basis for mutual help?
Given the different types of networks to which she belonged, Mrs.
Dewar could probably arrange a meeting with the county director
of manpower. Should Mrs. Dewar proceed, as she very much
wanted to? At that time, it was not easy to answer the question. It
would require time for Mrs. Dewar to get through to the director
and brief him on the network's existence, rationale, and activities;
if a meeting were arranged it would require Sarason, Davies, and
Reppucci to give a day (New Haven is fifty-five miles from Mrs.
Dewar's community) to such a meeting; the director may be unin-
terested, but come to a meeting because of her status; that is, the
meeting may very well be a waste of time. She decided to proceed.
The New Haven contingent came to the meeting somewhat re-
luctantly. The meeting was refreshing in several respects. Mr. K.,
the director, made no bones about the political origins and nature
of his position; he was dissatisfied with existing manpower programs
and was looking for new ideas and approaches; he could handle
himself well in the realm of ideas and concepts; he was intrigued
with what we were trying to do; and yes he wanted to come to our
meetings and try to be helpful, as well as to enlist help. At a much
later date, Mr. K. reported his perceptions of that meeting. Paraphrased, it went this way: "None of you wanted anything for your-
selves and that was refreshingly odd. I didn't quite understand
what the network concept was, but I did understand immediately
that what you were after was breaking down the walls between
agencies, and it is by banging against those walls that I have become bloodied. But what really got me was after the meeting when
I realized that for the first time in months I had been discussing
ideas! Day and night I am running, *doing* things, but really not
thinking."[4] Mr. K. attended more network meetings than we had

[4] Almost without exception, Mrs. Dewar had a meeting or some
form of communication with each person whom we were seeking to bring
into the network. She would explain the network's purposes and scope and
indicate who its members were. But, as we said earlier, one must never
assume that these communications have been appropriately comprehended.
After all, words are mischievous vehicles for mutual understanding. It is in
the context of the meetings that the significance of "give and get," the
conceptual aspect of the network's rationale, begins to change the imagery or
expectations that individuals had through prior communications.

reason to expect. It would take a separate chapter to describe the several ways by which Mr. K. tried to obtain resources to enlarge the network so that it interconnected with some of his programs and could serve as a demonstration to the county about how resources can be viewed and utilized more productively at surprisingly little cost. But the monies he controlled were earmarked so as to make this impossible.

We have described how Mr. K. joined the network, as an example of what went on in "meetings between meetings." But it is an instance of an activity of that very small group who felt and assumed responsibility for all that happened. The fact is that as the general network meetings became regular affairs, occurring six or so times a year, and the size of the network increased (creating the problem of where twenty-five to thirty people could meet comfortably), there were numerous "meetings between meetings" of different permutations and combinations of network members. It would be relatively easy for us to present charts describing the quantitative growth of the network in two ways. First, we could trace growth in terms of the number of people who participated, type of participation, frequency of participation, and how each of these participants varied in the degree to which they acted as interconnectors with other networks. When we talked earlier of meetings of twenty-five to thirty participants, we did not mean that that represented the extent of the actual network. Far from it. For example, there were three people from the somewhat geographically distant college of education who considered themselves active network members, in the sense that they were or wished to be actively engaged in projects with other network members. Rarely did all three come to a general network meeting. The same was true of the Yale group.

We could also get up charts showing the *possible* interconnections that could be forged over time between each active participant and relevant individuals and agencies in others of his or her networks. Just to try to chart these possibilities for Mrs. Dewar would take pages, and for most other people in the active network the number of pages would be less but still impressive. And if you put them all together, the New York phone book might well be dwarfed by comparison. More important than these chartings or quantifications is the degree to which over time it becomes second nature to active participants to be sensitive to possibilities, that is, to see and make interconnections. In getting up very complicated charts, there is always the danger of confusing quality with quantity, action as a value in itself with action consistent with purpose. Charts tell us little about process and purpose and too frequently they give the impression of an unwarranted degree of rationality and linearity.

In principle, we are not opposed to charts and systematic quantification, and we have absolutely no doubt that for certain purposes they are important and necessary. But like all techniques (statistical and otherwise) their use rests on certain judgments about how well different techniques serve one's purposes. Our purpose has been to describe how certain values, ideas, and goals gave rise to actions, the problems we encountered in action, and the complexity of describing these actions and some of their consequences. Consequently, in this section, in which we have been describing "meetings between meetings," we wished to convey how these meetings were outgrowths of previous general meetings and sometimes had no direct relationship to any previous general meeting. Some of these inbetween meetings were planned; others were not. There was one other very important function of some of these meetings: planning the timing of and agenda for the next general meeting. Timing and agenda are not simple matters. What happens at these meetings, how it happens, the momentum it gives to network activity, the degree to which awareness of the network's purposes is heightened, the deepening of the sense of community—given all these factors, we have learned to regard the general meeting as crucial to the viability of the network. More correctly, the general meeting contains the best data relevant to the question about the consistency between network purposes and activities. Because of its importance, we devote the next chapter to the general meeting.

The Triuniversity Network

How do networks grow? How do networks interconnect? There is more than one answer to these questions and we have tried to indicate some of them in our description of the Essex network.

In this section, we will again confront these questions, but this time from the perspective of social history and certain social and educational programs. To describe the Essex network is one thing; to understand its rationale, characteristics, and growth requires that we turn our attention away from the Essex network, from its immediate past, present, and future, to a series of federal programs ultimately and unpredictably fateful for the Essex network. If you think of the Essex network as if it were a child, our description thus far has neglected some of its important genealogy. If the mechanism of transmission was not genes but people, social forces rather than "the family," we can neglect genealogy only at the expense of a broader understanding of the Essex network.

The story involves a series of programs begun in the mid-nineteen sixties and conceived, administered, and supported by the U.S. Office of Education. When we say *support,* we mean hundreds of millions of dollars over a period of years. The story has been told in numerous publications (Bigelow, 1971; Provus, 1975; Merrow, Foster, and Estes, 1974), and we only present here in skeleton fashion those aspects that turned out to influence the origins, nature, and development of the Essex network. For the sake of brevity and clarity, we will very briefly describe aspects of the skeleton of what is in truth a fantastically complicated history.

First, one of the major thrusts of the U.S. Office of Education in the sixties was to devise and support ways of breaking down the walls between schools and community. The schools were being blamed (scapegoated?) for many of society's problems at the same time they were being asked to solve those problems. From within and without schools, pressure mounted to alter the school-community relationships, that is, to make schools more responsive to community needs and opinions (Sarason, 1976b).

A second thrust stemmed from the recognition that, just as school-community relationships had to change, so did the relationships between school personnel and the colleges and universities where they received their professional preparation. If school personnel were unduly insulated from the community, and unable to adapt (educationally and attitudinally) to the needs of their students, it reflected the inadequacy of their professional training. Criticism took two forms: Teachers were not sufficiently well grounded in the subject matter they taught, and they lacked an appreciation of and sensitivity to the cultural, historical, political, racial, and economic characteristics of our society and its communities.

Third, criticism of schools of education and undergraduate teacher training programs was pointed and strong. More muted (or more diffuse) was criticism of the liberal arts core of higher education. In its own way, it had stood apart from and looked down on the professional educator in particular and the field of education in general. So, it was not only a problem of altering the relationships *between school and university,* of making each more knowledgeable about and responsive to the other, but of altering in the same way relationships *within the university. It was even more complicated than that because altering these relationships had to be seen in the context of altering, again in the same ways, school-community relationships.* As one wag put it: "It isn't that the left hand does not know what the right hand is doing. That's bad enough. It is that it doesn't *want* to know." Each of the parties in this social drama needed each other but none of them seemed to want each other.

Fourth, it is senseless to argue about who in the Office of Education first began to see the problem whole, or what outside people and forces exerted pressure on that office to move it in new directions. The fact is that at least one person became absorbed, if not possessed, by the problems and sought and was given a leadership role in the Office of Education: Donald Bigelow, an historian from academia who decided to become part of the effort to improve the quality of education. A charismatic, provocative, provoking, tireless, concept-generating individual, he started to think of programs that would begin to put the pieces together: the community, schools, and different parts of the universities. Like Mrs. Dewar, Bigelow seemed to know everybody, or at least enough people who could give him access to everybody. And, like Mrs. Dewar, he seemed naturally to see the world in both its interconnectedness and the strength of forces and barriers making mutuality an empty term of rhetoric.

Fifth, infrequently at first, and with dim awareness of its significance, Bigelow began to employ a concept of networks as a way of describing what he was after. He knew that the easy part of the task was bringing the pieces together. The difficult task was to keep them together. It is fair to say that Bigelow never developed a differentiated conception of how this could be done. In part, this was due to the simple fact that in those days the "feds" had little or no time to think through anything (Sarason, 1976b). Between the pressures stemming from Congress' style of legislating and funding, those emanating from the equally complex cauldron in the executive branch, and those emanating from citizens and groups around the country, the major problem was how to spend the money. Thinking time was a luxury item nowhere entered in the budget. There was another factor: There were few people, if any, who could have been of practical help to Bigelow. (In fact, one source of his disillusion-ment was the recognition of how little of practical value the aca-demic community had to offer educational policy makers.) In any event, *networks* became an "in" word; not, however, an "in" con-cept, because that would suggest that thinking went beyond the idea or hope that if one brought people together, social chemistry would somehow forge lasting and productive relationships. Bigelow was aware of the limitations of his concept of networks, as he was that his cries for help availed him little.

Sixth, Bigelow was aware of one other crucial factor, one that was the source of his power or influence as well as a subversive obstacle to his goals. He had lots of money, and this meant that he would have little difficulty in getting the different groups to meet, plan, and act. It also meant that one had to be somewhat skeptical of the sincerity of the motivation of some of these individuals and groups. They would meet, they would plan, they would agree to cooperate, but, in practice, would traditional self-interest give way to the hoped-for mutuality? Would there be a thin facade of co-operation hiding individual, agency, or institutional aggrandize-ment? What would happen when the monies ran out? Unfortunately, the answers were frequently in line with fears. Money, especially if it is sizable, can be a powerful spur to creative thinking about how to get it, act, and still maintain the status quo.

Seventh, a relatively large number of people were part of Bigelow's personal and professional network, and it was a network based not on money, but on friendship, intellectual compatibility, shared experiences, and a willingness to be available to Bigelow and each other. Sarason was part of that network, in part because he had been drawn in (like Mrs. Dewar, Bigelow was a very persuasive and persistent person) to several projects that Bigelow's branch was supporting, and also because he admired and respected what Bigelow was trying to do. Far closer to Bigelow and much more involved in the planning and execution of different projects and programs was Saul Cohen, Director of the Graduate School of Geography at Clark University.

Eighth, generally speaking, Bigelow's efforts fell far short of their goals and no one agonized more about why this happened, what lessons could be learned, than Bigelow. Sarason and Cohen were similarly trying to make sense out of their experiences with Bigelow. Sarason began to relate these experiences to those which he and his colleagues had with a very diverse array of community agencies. Cohen decided to seek funding to accomplish two major goals: to bring together individuals from three universities who were interested in studying the concept of networks, and who would become the core, so to speak, of a network exemplifying what they had learned and formulated. This was the triuniversity network (Clark, Yale, and State University of New York [SUNY] at Stony Brook).

The triuniversity network was activated a year after the Essex network. It will be recalled that in that previous year, the Essex network consisted of several people (Dewar, Sarason, Davies, Reppucci) encountering numerous dead ends in their search for tie-ins with different agencies. So when the triuniversity network began, Sarason and Reppucci were common to both networks, neither of which was going anywhere in particular. Indeed, the initial meetings of the triuniversity network were somewhat embarrassing affairs, even though each participant knew each other and with one exception had been part of one or another of Bigelow's projects. Unlike the Essex network, which was explicitly action oriented from the start, the triuniversity network was initially a study group on networks. That is to say, initially it had the characteristics of a group rather than a network and the early meetings of such groups are not easy affairs. There was one other factor to which we have alluded in our description of Bigelow's efforts: All of the participants in the triuniversity network were academicians who had spent their lives treasuring their autonomy. As a group, academicians are not noted for mutuality in their relationships. After all, individuals who seek careers in the university are individualists, and the university selects its faculty on the basis of *individual accomplishment.* Is the university justified, therefore, in its frequent complaint that faculty do not cooperate as much as they should? We point this out not only to illustrate the obstacles in tradition and personal style a network based on mutuality has to overcome in the university, but also to suggest that the university is an unusually clear example of what is true throughout our society.

We shall have more to say about the triuniversity network in later chapters. At this point, what the reader needs to know is that for several months after it was organized, there was no attempt to interconnect it in any way with the Essex network. This was deliberate on the part of Sarason and Reppucci, who believed that because one could interconnect two networks was not reason enough to do so. The timing and the occasion had to be considered. Sarason and Reppucci would be hard put to state clearly the basis for their judgments, but it went something like this: You had to avoid a meeting in which one person had to spend a good deal of time talking *to* other people telling them about their experiences and purposes, a meeting that may be relevant for biographical purposes but not for sensing communality of needs and thought, and it should be a meeting around concrete issues of action, allowing participants in a more natural or less formal way to reflect their needs, thoughts, and style. Furthermore, in the case of these two networks, there was the reality of distance: Stony Brook and Clark University were more distant from Essex than even Yale.

The interconnection took place at a triuniversity meeting devoted to a discussion of the monograph *Youth: Transition to Adulthood,* a report of the Panel on Youth of the President's Science Advisory Committee (1973). It has also been called the "Coleman II" report because the monograph was the work of a committee chaired by James Coleman, who had a similar role in the earlier, much discussed and influential *Equality of Educational Opportunity* (1966). It was the second report that recommended that the walls between the world of school and work be broken down and that high school youth should spend a significant portion of the school year in work settings. To the triuniversity people these recommendations, if taken seriously, would confront all of the issues and obstacles met by Bigelow in his efforts to develop more productive interconnections among school, community, and centers of higher education. Unfortunately, the report showed no sensitivity to these issues or obstacles, that is, to what would be required if the resources of the school and community were to take on new forms of exchange. Invited to this meeting were people from labor unions, school administration, high school principals and teachers. In all, there were twenty-five people at the meeting. Mrs. Dewar was also invited, with two results: Cohen recognized the communalities between Mrs. Dewar and himself, and Mrs. Dewar recognized that there were "resources" at that meeting who could be very valuable to her efforts. From that point on, the overlap between the two networks steadily increased.

We cannot describe in comprehensive detail all of the productive interconnections made as a result of that meeting. (Nor can we discuss how the substance of the discussion at that meeting confirmed our already strong feeling that the major recommendations of the Coleman II report were at best superficial, and at worst irresponsible, in not discussing what the implementation of the recommendations would encounter, or in indicating in outline what a viable strategy would be. Needless to say, from our standpoint, important aspects of that strategy would require a differentiated conception of networks, resources, and resource exchange.) But one of these interconnections deserves description for two reasons: It was unexpected and it led to a sustained relationship of Cohen and his students with the Essex network.

To most people, a geographer or geography is concerned with maps. The truth is that geography has become a field of wide scope, including land use, conservation, environmental protection, recreation and land use, issues surrounding human and material resources, ecology, and so on. Like practically every other field represented in a university, geography today is discernibly different than it was at the end of World War II. When, during and after the "Coleman II" meeting, Cohen and Mrs. Dewar got to know each other, he found out about her activities in environmental studies and also that in the local high school one of the teachers was providing some students with truly educational field experiences in data collection and processing in the field of earth studies. She found out about the scope of Cohen's interests and expertise, as well as his interest in finding stimulating field experiences for his graduate students. What probably solidified their relationship was this shared belief: *In any relationship involving a student (high school, college) in a community, the agency or community groups involved, the school, and the student all had to feel that the student was performing a needed function, not cheap or free labor, and that in providing the appropriate supervision for the student, it would be creating new roles for some of its own employees or for new kinds of employees that would be beneficial to the employees, agency, school, and students.* The problem, as Mrs. Dewar and Cohen recognized, was in society's view of students as incapable of performing a socially useful community function—in regard to this point, the Coleman II report could not be more clear and correct.

As we indicated, environmental education had been an Essex network interest of the science teacher in the local high school, who had been supervising students in monitoring changes in the nearby reservoir. Network members helped in different ways this innovative, action-oriented teacher to expand his program. Significant among these efforts was the encouragement to forge a relationship with a quite distant state university that had highly qualified faculty in the earth sciences. In exchange for faculty expertise and use of sophisticated equipment, the program would provide students from this university access to field sites in the Essex area as well as opportunities to work with high school students and teachers.

But there was a problem. The science teacher was eager that the findings from the students' studies be communicated to and used by local communities. The problem inhered in the fact that, according to proliferating county and state ecological study guidelines, only research done by highly certified specialists could be used for administrative or practical or policy-making purposes. Volunteer groups could be involved in limited ways. In order to help the science teacher as well as to clarify the issues and possibly to seek changes in the interpretation of regulations, Mrs. Dewar arranged a meeting to which Cohen came with two colleagues, one of whom was a former conservation director for the Army Corps of Engineers. Also present at the meeting were representatives from the high school, the regional division of vocational education, the area's conservation board, a local nonprofit nature conservancy, and the local program of the federally funded program in environmental education. The main question discussed at that meeting was whether it was possible to train high school and adult volunteers to carry out ecological studies that ordinarily required high-priced specialists. This in no way meant that anyone was recommending doing away with specialists, who in any event were not numerous enough to do all that needed to be done, but, simply, was there a mutually rewarding, socially useful role for students and adult volunteers and possibly a new role for experts in their training and supervision? Aside from solidifying the Clark contingent's participation in the Essex network, the meeting was quite important in terms of changing attitudes about the use of students and adult volunteers.[5]

Concurrent with this crucial meeting, some other developments were brewing in regard to environmental education. The reader will recall that several members of a graduate college of education were active members of the network, especially in regard to day-care programs (for example, inservice training, community participation, self-help programs). Through them, the Essex network was made known to one of their faculty members who had been asked to develop the educational program of a large state park that was to involve the school districts of five counties. He had numerous conversations with Mrs. Dewar and he asked her to link him with members of Essex school districts who might be interested. She arranged a meeting for him to present his program. She also invited to the meeting William R. Eblen, Director of Total Educa-

---

[5] This does not mean that we were successful in getting regulations changed so that the studies by students and adult volunteers could be used. These studies continued to be carried out, of course, but they were used as a basis for community education for students. Both adults and high school students gave part of their energies to taking advantage of the community participation "clauses" in federal regulations. For the science teacher and his students who, heretofore, saw themselves as "scientists," their experience with the dilemmas and opportunities of application considerably broadened their understanding of the relationship between research and social action. Far from the students remaining in the traditional, isolated role of students, they in fact learned about and became part of their community.

tion in the Total Environment (TETE), to describe his program and to show a film about his national and international work. Not only did she hope that a relationship could be established between Eblen and the college faculty member, since she saw shared educational approaches, but also between each of their organizations and the Essex network. This meeting went extremely well. It led to another meeting to forward the college faculty member's program, hosted by the regional director of educational services (a network member) who saw various ways in which programs in different school districts could benefit from what the faculty member's project had to offer.

But the meeting had more implications than that. Through TETE, Mr. and Mrs. Eblen had conducted workshops for fifty state departments of education as well as similar ministries in various developing nations. The Eblens were part of an extensive international network, including many of the world's leading environmentalists. Indeed, TETE had strong support in the United Nations and was seeking foundation support to set up demonstration centers in different ecological settings around the globe. When the Eblens understood the Essex network's rationale, they saw it as conceptually important to their goals and strategies. Another meeting, of the Eblens and the Yale and Clark contingents, was held specifically on networking concepts and their applicability to TETE. Cohen was crucial at this meeting, not only because of his views on networking, but also because of his own international experience in matters of the environment. At the end of the meeting, there was obvious agreement about many things, not the least of which was that we had a great deal to give and get from each other. Shortly after that meeting, the Eblens did receive foundation support and were giving serious consideration to the Essex area, not only as a headquarters but as one of the demonstration sites. At the time we are writing, the matter has not been finally resolved, but the interconnections between Cohen, Dewar, the Eblens, and a number of members of the Essex and other networks have been made and are ongoing in diverse ways around diverse projects.

The triuniversity network was not, despite the title of this section, our main focus, but rather a means by which we could convey and emphasize several points. First, both networks were, in part at least, descendants of large but ill-fated federal programs sparked by Bigelow who helped give the word *network* wide currency. Bigelow's efforts provided experiences to Cohen and Sarason that were important to their thinking. Second, we wanted to indicate when and under what conditions networks "consciously" interconnect, and with what consequences. We put quotes around *consciously* because, although interconnections can come about in strange and unpredictable kinds of ways—and they probably are the most frequent ways—we wished to underline why seeking interconnections sometimes requires planning and attention to timing. Third, we wished to have a basis for suggesting that the productiveness of interconnections is in part a function not only of the perception of mutual self-interest, but of common values as well. Fourth, we wished to underline the obvious point that when two networks interconnect the opportunities for either of them to connect with other networks, and even for all of these networks to form interrelationships, are increased dramatically. This was the reason we focused on the relationships between the two networks in regard to environmental education, because, in a relatively short period of time, other networks, near and far, were drawn in and a whole new set of sustained interrelationships emerged. We shall reserve for a later chapter what this means for the deceptively simple questions: What is a network? What are its boundaries? In the case of the Essex network, we have already indicated that one of its characteristics was its "self-appointed" core group, which by this point in the story consisted of Mrs. Dewar, Sarason, and Cohen. To further the reader's understanding of this, and indirectly to begin to answer the two deceptively simple questions, we turn in the next chapter to the nature and functions of the general network meeting, a kind of town hall.

6

The Functions of the
General Meeting

There are usually about four to six general meetings a year. Between two general meetings there is a score or so of smaller meetings, the number of participants varying from two to a dozen. The smaller meetings are almost always a consequence of the general meeting. Although in this chapter we shall focus on the general meeting, its functions and predictable problems, we do not intend a sharp dichotomy between it and other meetings. There are differences between the two types of meetings, but there is also overlap.

Purposes

One of the main purposes of the general meeting is to report to the network members about what went on since the last meeting;

more correctly, to give the different subgroups an opportunity to tell about their activities so as to elicit ideas and broader participation. Because there are different groups organized around different activities, the general meeting must be the main vehicle to provide some sense of being part of a larger community. From our perspective, it is not enough that each of the different subgroups has cohered as a group and has even become interconnected with other networks. That is cause for satisfaction, but if these subgroups "go their own way," they rob themselves and the rest of the network of a sense of common origins and of belonging to a larger, mutually supporting network community. Equally important, by reporting back to the general meeting, other as well as new network members frequently are able to see ways by which they can interconnect with another subgroup.

Another major purpose of the general meeting is to provide visitors and new members the opportunity to meet other members and to glean something of the network's diversity of people and activities. Describing the network, as we have stressed, is no easy matter, and although the general meeting by no means answers all of an individual's questions, it does convey facts and characteristics that give substance to verbal description. For example, at any general meeting there will be at least a half dozen (of twenty-five to thirty) people who have come from long distances; the array of roles and agencies represented at a meeting is very heterogeneous; and few decisions are ever made at these meetings. It is not among the purposes of the meeting to be a decision-making occasion. (A vote has never been taken.) Rather, the meeting is intended to be "opportunity revealing" in the sense that, from the reports and discussion, new possibilities are presented to the participants. In previous chapters, we have emphasized the unpredictability of network activity and development, and this unpredictability is also a characteristic of the general meeting. This is not only due to the fact that the reports contain new information or that new people express themselves from different experiences and perspectives. Equally important, we believe, is that people are there voluntarily, that is, they have been there before and they have returned, the intrinsic motivation to participate is strong.

Without question, the most important *implicit* purpose of

the general meeting is a didactic one. That is to say, the meeting must illustrate and discuss the rationale for the network's existence: new ways of viewing and using resources, expanding and differentiating one's perception of one's self and others, and forging a sense of belonging in a mutually supportive way to a widening circle of people. This does not mean that you state this rationale or lecture about it in a "for virtue and against sin" way. What it does mean is that one has to be unusually vigilant for those moments in the meeting when the point or points can be made casually, that is, when one senses that one is putting into words what people are thinking. This, of course, is easier said than done. But the difficulties in doing it, let alone doing it well, are no warrant for avoiding it. After all, what is at stake is the consistency between activities and their underlying rationale. What cannot be overemphasized or lost sight of is how strong are the centrifugal forces within our society and, therefore, in us. In our working roles, we are not accustomed to deal with others on a barter exchange basis. This may even be more true for agencies than for individuals but since as working individuals we are usually part of agencies, the insularity of agencies constricts the individual's opportunities for a different state of affairs. Nor can we underestimate how the quantity and quality of interpersonal relationships are influenced by differences in profession, status, age, perceived affluence, and so on. Like it or not, there are pecking orders within and between individuals and agencies, and they almost always make for one-way rather than two-way types of interpersonal roads. And, of course, ours is an explicitly individualistic, competitive society that has built into us the "heads I win, tails you lose" stance. We are set to see this stance in others far more than we see it in ourselves. None of us is exempt from these influences. Therefore, in forming the network, we knew that combatting these influences would be no easy matter. Moreover, these were not problems to be solved in a once-and-for-all manner; they would have to be dealt with as ever-present problems.

We came to see the general meeting as crucial to our purposes. This does not mean that the "meetings between meetings" were less important or that they had very different purposes. But, unlike the general meetings, these other meetings tended to be more task oriented and have a decision-making character. They usually were consequences of the general meeting, a coming together of a few people to explore further and to decide about a joint venture that emerged as a possibility at the general meeting. As time went on, however, some of these smaller groups took on a life or direction of their own, interconnecting with other networks, and capable, so to speak, of taking care of themselves. This, of course, was quite consistent with certain aspects of the network rationale but inconsistent with that part concerned with the sense of common origins and community. The general meeting is the only vehicle by which to combat such inconsistency. In this type of network, people are free to come and go, to be a part or not to be a part, and to participate a little or a lot. Without the centripetal influence of the general meeting, one of our important purposes could not be realized.

The reader may be asking, "Who are 'we'?" On what basis did "we" take on responsibility for others in certain ways? Whose network is it? How do we know that "our" purposes become those of others? We shall deal with the last question later in this chapter. A general answer would be that ours is a network that has a self-conscious, self-appointed core group endeavoring to wed theory and practice. But that answer is from the perspective of the core group. How do network members see the network? From their perspective, the network is not only Mrs. Dewar's idea but she is the force keeping it going, that is, she has created the conditions that have introduced the members to new people, ideas, and possibilities. However, that perception has undergone a subtle change since the first year or so of the network's existence. As the network grew in people and activities, and as each of the different subgroups organized around a particular interest, the centrality of Mrs. Dewar's role has been somewhat diminished. She is still perceived as *the* directing force, she arranges for and chairs the general meetings, and, more than anyone else, she initiates contacts with network members; but, as the subgroups have developed a commitment to their particular interests, they inevitably experience what may be termed a *divided loyalty* effect. This is an understandable and even desirable state of affairs, but it creates a problem for the general meeting, which is the one occasion when the rationale for the relationship between parts and whole can be experienced. In short, she was *accorded* the role of leader or director as much as she is *ex-pected* to do so. Initially, people described it as *her* network; after two years one hears members talk of *our* or *the* network.

Problems of the General Meeting

If we look at the general meeting in terms of its preparation, it is quickly apparent that the first problem is a consequence of agenda making. In a formal organization for which the locus of administrative and legal responsibility is usually quite clear, it is both easy and frequent for leaders to determine what the agenda of a general meeting will be. In the Essex network, which is in-formal and voluntary and requires for its viability the sustaining of a strong, self-determined desire to participate, the agenda must reflect the opinions and advice of members. If they willingly come to the meetings, it is because (in part) it has in some way become their meeting, not someone else's, for example, Mrs. Dewar's. That sounds easy and virtuous until one realizes that the number of active participants in the network makes such surveying an im-possibility. Even if one restricts the survey to the twenty-five to thirty people who most consistently attend general meetings, the survey of advice and opinion can be quite time consuming. This has not been as difficult a problem as it might be, because Mrs. Dewar tries to make it her business to know what goes on in "meetings be-tween meetings." But one is still left with the question of deciding what agenda items should be included on the basis that they appear best to serve the immediate and long-term purposes of the network. And if one is as conscious as one should be about planning a pro-ductive meeting, which will include the main interests of each member, decisions about the agenda should never be easy. In a formal, hierarchically structured organization, there may be a desire to have interesting meetings, but it is rarely a source of concern.

Rarely has the agenda been covered (or even largely covered) at a meeting.[1] This is a mixed blessing, because at the same time that it indicates the interest aroused by the early agenda

---

[1] These meetings begin at 10 A.M., break for an hour's buffet lunch, and go to 2 P.M. The meetings are held in a room of an agency (school, college, residential institution) of a network member.

items, the articulateness of many of the participants, and the lack of pressure to cover the agenda, it also means that agenda items of special concern to some members never get discussed, and it is understandable if they feel in some way shortchanged. After all, if you have come to a meeting expecting or hoping to discuss or raise an issue, and the opportunity to do so never comes up, you should feel disappointed. And such disappointment is not assuaged easily by the fact that discussion may have a rambling character that often is heady, stimulating, and even exciting, in terms of network opportunities. In addition, because at any general meeting there usually are observers or potential members to whom questions are directed, or who enter the discussion from their particular perspective (personal or agency), the amount of discussion time available to network members is reduced.

These are not minor matters. The general meetings are not frequent and yet they are a major vehicle through which members learn about what has been happening, and what may or should be happening. They also serve a socially and intellectually welding function. Therefore, what members experience at the meeting, the satisfactions or dissatisfactions they derive from it, are important factors in determining the strength of their motivation to continue in the network and, fatefully, their willingness to articulate their perception of the consistency between network rationale and activities (substance and style). Interacting with all of this are two "predispositions" that should never be underestimated. First, the network rationale and its completely voluntary character run counter to what we are ordinarily accustomed to in working meetings, a fact commented on by newer participants. On two different occasions, for example, individuals remarked with some surprise how unusual it was to attend meetings where money was not discussed, comments suggesting how prepotent is the tendency to be on guard to protect and serve one's interests. The other predisposition is to expect that meetings will be decision-making affairs where organizational and procedural matters are taken up. At almost every general meeting, we now expect at least one individual to complain that there is too much discussion, too many ideas and opportunities, and too little focus or decisions. The general meeting is not task oriented, in the sense that we do not discuss problems and seek to decide how to solve them. Rather, the general meeting focuses on issues, and it is a forum to discuss the diverse opportunities they present to the network's purposes and activities. This is not to say that decisions are forbidden or never made, but that discussions are primarily an effort deliberately to examine the diverse ways members may relate themselves to the possibility at hand. Strong in most of us is the tendency to value "making decisions" or "coming to the point" more than extended, rambling discussions of possibilities. As one member said: "The discussions are *really* interesting, but I have the feeling they don't get us very far." We are tempted to suggest that the more decisions made at a meeting, or that the more discussion there is about what decision to make, the less interesting a meeting is. It is our belief that what has kept a relatively large number of people returning to general meetings is that the meetings are interesting. For some people, they are both interesting and frustrating.

If we are stressing the importance of interesting meetings, it is not because we overevaluate talk or the importance of giving people an opportunity to think about and respond to possibilities for action. It is because, from our perspective, a meeting is interesting because it fulfills the following network objectives: It illustrates how the network rationale has been implemented, it confronts the implications of new possibilities, it facilitates exposure to new people and ideas, and it gratifies people's need for a sense of noncompetitive common purpose, as well as for a sense of being part of an extended community of people. One never meets these objectives in a wholly satisfactory manner, and in addition to the obstacles we have already mentioned there is one that stems from the burden put on the meeting's moderator (Mrs. Dewar), who must be extraordinarily sensitive to the general ambience of the meeting, to what people are saying or not saying, to explicit or implicit criticisms, to *her* need to participate and to her obligation to facilitate the participation of others, and to when one should try to move the discussion in a certain direction or try to terminate it. But over and beyond these considerations, the moderator must be set to capitalize on those unpredictable moments and statements that allow the purposes of the network to be articulated, that is, to remind everyone that the substance of the discussion cannot be understood only by what is being said or done in the "here and now" of the discussion but has to be seen in terms of specific network objectives. The discussion and the activities giving rise to it are, so to speak, like the melodic line we are aware of when we listen to a symphony. But the discussion, like the melodic line, has a "ground" of which we are frequently unaware. When we hear the opening theme of a symphony, we do not realize that the way in which we experience it is in part determined by the fact that most of the instruments are not playing the theme, but nevertheless are influencing how we hear it. Similarly, in the flow of the meeting we pay attention first to one concrete issue, then to another, and on and on, usually unaware that what we are attending to or talking about has a history as well as a structure in the present of which we are usually unaware. If the general meeting is in an explicit way not for the purpose of making decisions, it *is* in an explicit way intended to help us see the relationships between figure and ground, that is, between rationale and principles, on the one hand, and activities and talk, on the other hand.

If in the conduct of the general meeting Mrs. Dewar sometimes falls short of the mark, it should occasion no surprise. For a general meeting to be run well requires a kind of radar not very many people have. To gloss over this fact is to misrepresent reality and to oversimplify egregiously the problems in the general meeting. What has been helpful to Mrs. Dewar has been her discussions with Sarason and Cohen before and after each meeting (at which one or both have almost always been present). As important as the help given by Sarason and Cohen is Mrs. Dewar's awareness that preparing for and reflecting on a meeting are too important and complex (and too fateful for the network's viability) to be one person's responsibility. The general meeting is unlike most others we encounter in our lives and its distinctiveness resides as much in its conduct as it does in its purposes. It has some of the characteristics of a town hall meeting, a revival missionary occasion, a family circle meeting, college seminar, alumni reunion, and an exercise in brainstorming. These characteristics may not sit well with some people (as they do not with some network members), and they may not be appropriate or valid, but at the very least they may convey what we wish to convey: The general meeting is a rather strange affair, until you have been to several of them and in the interval between meetings have engaged in network activity.

Given the growth of the network in terms of people and activities, the point has been reached where the general meeting can no longer serve in the desired way some of its purposes. It cannot meaningfully keep members well informed about all the activities going on and face-to-face contact among all participants is difficult if not impossible. Growth, as we know, is a mixed blessing and it can be an unalloyed evil if quantitative aspects divert attention from its qualitative ones. We can take satisfaction from the growth of the Essex network, but the point has been reached where one thing is certain: There are people in the network who are strangers to each other, which is a way of saying that a limit has been reached to some people's sense of belonging to an extended community. Inevitably there is *a* limit and the practical question is whether as matters now stand the present limits can be somewhat extended. It is our opinion that we have not given sufficient attention to this question, although, as we shall see in the next section, the question has by no means been bypassed.

The Coordinator

After two years it became apparent that too much was going on—and that a lot more yet could be going on—for Mrs. Dewar to coordinate. Although a private citizen, she did have other interests and responsibilities. To prepare for and moderate general meetings occupied a small part of her time. Far more time consuming was following through on "opportunities for barter": contacting (by letter, phone, visit) people, arranging for small meetings, attending them, and being helpful to these small groups in whatever ways were possible. She was a perfect catalyst, but in addition she had a very clear idea about the catalytic process that went way beyond merely bringing people together. So, when it became obvious that the Essex network was becoming more extended (interpersonally and geographically) and that the time she could give to the network would not be sufficient, a full-time coordinator was needed.

What does one look for in a coordinator? What should such

a person know or be prepared to learn? Is it necessary that such a person have some kind of professional training and credentials? If yes, in what discipline is such a person likely to be found? Since the coordinator in the Essex network has no power, what personality or temperament characteristics does one look for? How does one "break in" such a person to a new role so that, like any other network member, some kind of desirable balance is struck between his or her purposes and those of others? How is the definition and choice of a coordinator a test of the network's rationale?

The word *coordinator* is often employed to avoid the impression that the person is in a leadership role, that is, coordination is not leadership, it is not based on granted powers, or, at least, on very little formal power. As we have made clear, for more than a year Mrs. Dewar had functioned both as leader and coordinator, her force residing not in formally granted power, but in the attractiveness of her ideas and personal style. In seeking a coordinator, we were not looking for someone to be her appendage or office clerk, but someone who could develop (like Mrs. Dewar) into a leader and coordinator role; more accurately, someone who, like her, would earn influence through performance. But, as we emphasized in an earlier chapter, quality or excellence is in limited supply in any role or work. We also could assume that few people would be available to us who independently had formulated something akin to the network's rationale. So we were faced with a dilemma: The person we chose must have leadership qualities, but that person would have to work, for some time at least, under Mrs. Dewar's tutelage. Put in another way, the coordinator would be unlike any other member of the network whose degree and style of participation had no external constraints. We were quite aware that one of the danger points in the growth of any social unit is the "stranger," and this was peculiarly salient to the Essex network, given its emphasis on mutuality. Choosing a person is one thing. Creating the appropriate conditions for his growth consistent with the network's reason for being is quite another thing. If we emphasize these problems, it is not to labor the obvious, but to suggest that the obvious is rarely taken seriously.

But what should this person know or learn? The answer, of course, is what Mrs. Dewar knew and had learned. That is literally impossible, because each person is unique in that his experiences, their organization, and his style are not replicable. But even if it were possible, is it desirable? We did not view her as a model of perfection in her role of leader and coordinator, nor did she. It is possible to state and strive, to grasp and implement what she stood for: each of us lives in a social and physical environment, our knowledge of and sensitivity to which are ordinarily constricted and dulled, so that we are unable to "mine" well this total resource for our own differentiated growth, just as our contributions to that resource remain potential rather than actual. In her own words: "Energies are imprisoned rather than released." Such a conception may sound vague and general, but in terms of perception and action it led to unusual clarity about what one had to know about people, institutions, and the environment; how things ordinarily worked, and how they ought to work. In the realm of knowledge, Mrs. Dewar was a *generalist*, not a specialist. A coordinator cannot be confined by the ordinary blinders of his or her professional specialty. Indeed, the more we thought about the coordinator's role, the more we saw the possibility that professionalization of the role, or deliberately seeking a person with professional credentials, could result in a transformation of the role to one of a narrow parochialism. This unintended result, as the Levines (1970) demonstrated so well in *Social History of Helping Services,* has been a frequent one. The danger we feared was in its own way a symptom of what the Essex network was intended to overcome. After all, it was primarily through Mrs. Dewar's efforts that network members (almost all of whom were professionals) learned to alter and enlarge their conceptions of themselves as resources and of the community as containing far more resources than they ever thought would be available to them. Her ability to see and arrange "matches" was a consequence of the fact that when she saw individuals and agencies she saw opportunities and possible interconnections. When one of our graduate students called her "Mrs. Gestalt," he was pinpointing an outlook she helped others to adopt. When she talked of the total environment, it was not a cliché or empty rhetoric or a token gesture to fashion. She is not antiprofessional or a derogator of standards, but neither is she blind to the narrowness of the professional's outlook.

What we sought, therefore, was a person who was not wedded to a narrow outlook, not absorbed with the technology of his or her training, was unafraid to venture into any or all aspects of community functioning, and had a personal style conducive to "matchmaking." We were seeking someone who could develop into a coordinator and leader, not just a bookkeeper or dispatcher or resource locator. The coordinator is a catalyst who, by virtue of his or her actions, produces and accelerates the exchange of resources; who constantly seeks new resources, not because a quantitative increase in a network is a virtue in itself, but because this increase introduces a new quality in the lives of the members.

We secured the services of a young, energetic man who had experience in stimulating community participation in school affairs. He had a master's degree in child psychology and had not pursued a doctorate because he concluded that its pursuit at this time in his life would be unduly confining. Like so many people his age, he felt unable to commit himself to one career line in which his need for diversity and roundedness would not be met (Sarason, 1977).[2] His major tasks were to work with Mrs. Dewar, learn the network rationale and its strategies, get to know the "territory," keep people better informed about network activities, and to keep people in better touch with each other. As we have said several times before, it is relatively easy to state the network rationale and to describe its activities, but comprehending verbal explanations must never be confused with understanding based on firsthand experience. It is the difference between telling a person about psychotherapy (or a movie, novel, and so on) and experiencing it for oneself. By his own account, it took him the better part of a year fully to comprehend and act appropriately on the rationale. It was not simply that he was much younger than Mrs. Dewar or lacked her status and experience, but rather that he had to struggle to refashion his perception of community resources and how one went

---

[2] It is worthy of note that the need of young people today for diversity, challenge, and the sense of personal growth is shared by older generations, except that the former more than the latter publicly articulate and act in accord with such a stance. The attractiveness of the Essex network to many of its "older" members is in the potential they see in it for the satisfaction of these needs.

about investigating and tapping them for network purposes. Also, it took time before he could truly grasp that he could count on most people, regardless of their status and credentials, to respond favorably to the network's rationale and their potential benefits from and contributions to the network. Whereas initially he had questions about how much time the role would require, he became no less busy than Mrs. Dewar as he grasped (and felt comfortable with) the implications of the rationale and could see consequences he had helped to produce. If there was any doubt in anyone's mind that a full-time coordinator was necessary, it was dispelled within a few months.

Ours has long been a society based on the myth of unlimited resources. We now know otherwise. The events of the past few years have demolished the myth, but it has also helped to engender a sense of impotence and hopelessness about how to think about, let alone deal with, the new set of circumstances. The concept of networks we have been describing represents one important conceptual approach to these circumstances. As will be apparent in the review of the literature, the concept of networks has been attracting attention in recent years and there is reason to believe that it will come more into center stage in coming decades. If we are right, and "networking" becomes fashionable as a way of thinking and acting, the concept of coordination and the role of coordinators will require the most thoughtful discussion. If we are to avoid mismanaging the growth of networks in the way we have done in so many aspects of growth in our society, coordination must not be viewed as a technical problem. If we again go that route, quantity remains quantity, with adverse consequences for quality. The goal, as Mrs. Dewar would put it, is to seek a quantitative growth that produces a qualitative change. The growth of a network does not necessarily mean that "we must be doing something right." It could mean that one has mindlessly fallen again into the morass of the numbers game. Lekachman (1970) has illustrated this well in regards to increases in the Gross National Product:

> The gross national product . . . is the total market value of the goods and services produced by our economy for a specified period of time, usually a year.

This quite representative definition is notable for its
utter neutrality. An unassuming man, the economist
makes no value judgments of his fellow citizens' tastes.
Whether the customers prefer the Beatles to Bach, foot-
ball to ballet, *Reader's Digest* to *Commentary*, or *Oh!
Calcutta!* to *Othello* is absolutely none of the national-
income analyst's professional business. Nor does his
private opinion gain force from his professional skills.
But this apparently harmless and even ingratiating
(scholars ought to be humble!) posture can be shown to
sanction some very odd and even ridiculous consequences.
Thus, if cigarette smoking were to double, the increase
would naturally show up as an expansion of the consumer component of the Gross National Product. And if
the corollary were a parallel rise in medical expenditure
for the treatment of lung cancer, tuberculosis, heart ail-
ments, and emphysema, this too would be solemnly added
to the GNP. If a new pulp mill discharges chemical
wastes into a hitherto clean stream, the GNP will go up,
not only because of the mill's valuable output but also
because other enterprises and municipalities located
downstream from the polluter will be compelled to invest
in cleansing devices required to return the water to
usable condition. Similarly, the GNP rises both with
automobile sales and with the increased consumer
expenditure for the cleaning of furniture, clothes, lungs,
and bodies, necessitated by such purchases.

For an Essex-type network to be beguiled by quantitative growth
would be a monumental irony. Precisely because the management
of the growth can be the most important problem confronting a
network, the role of the coordinator (or coordinators) has to be
seen for what it is: a strange mixture of knowledge, leadership, and
values, the influence of which derives not from formal power or
strength but from sheer palatability.

7

Funding and the Dilemmas of Growth

Consistent with the network's rationale, the many varieties of resource exchange the network has facilitated (directly or indirectly) have not involved money. That is to say, no discussion about resource exchange, or a later agreement on the part of members to share resources in some way, assumed some kind of money exchange among them. This, of course, does not mean that financial considerations were never in the picture, or that they introduced no constraints, or that seeking funds was considered an evil. What it does mean is that the network is an informal association of individuals, one of the major purposes of which is to help its members explore and pursue ways by which they could use each other in mutually productive ways. Participation is voluntary and the network has no money to give to anybody. If, in the process of working together, some members decide to seek funding to continue or to enlarge on what they had already done, that is their decision and responsibility, and they can call on the rest of the network for advice and help. For example, in Chapter Three we described several network activities that in one or another way involved school personnel. These were remarkably successful activities that will be continued, but precisely because of their consequences, some of the teachers wish to involve more students. To enlarge the scope would require very modest sums to free the teachers from some class periods. Efforts are being made by the teachers to obtain these funds ($3,000) but if their efforts are unsuccessful the activities will continue at their previous level. The important point is that these activities were conceived and carried out with available resources.

If people sought to meet and then work together, it was never because someone had money but rather because they saw an opportunity to exchange other types of resources. We have tried to make the reader aware that, geographically speaking, the Essex network became rather far-flung. University people from three states came to meetings. Leaving them aside, other members had to travel forty-five minutes to an hour one way to attend meetings. Travel expenses were an individual matter and responsibility. Some, not all, of these people had their own sources for reimbursement for travel, but that does not explain why they endeavored to come regularly to general or other meetings.

Because it is not a legal, corporate entity, the network cannot be given money, nor can it seek funds. This has created conceptual and administrative issues that are best discussed in terms of Mrs. Dewar's financial contributions to the network. They are not simple issues, because they force one to confront the network's rationale and the dilemmas of growth.

Mrs. Dewar's Financial Role

For the first two of the three years of the network's existence, Mrs. Dewar provided the buffet lunch for the general meetings. Food was simple, ample, and very edible. It would be brought into the room where the meeting was held, usually around noon, two hours after the general meeting had begun. At an appropriate point in the discussion, there would be a forty-five-minute break for lunch, during which time a good deal of business would get done: There were always visitors who would seek out certain members or be sought out by them for discussion; subgroups would form around "opportunities" that had come up at the morning's discussion; already formed subgroups would meet briefly around their common interests; dates and places for "meetings between meetings" would be arranged; and Mrs. Dewar, Sarason, and Cohen would usually meet briefly to share opinions about the morning meeting, as well as possible changes in the meeting after lunch. We do not wish to overevaluate the role of positive oral experiences, but neither do we wish to ignore the relationship between good food, good talk, and an ambience of camaraderie.

In addition, Mrs. Dewar paid a rather large phone bill. Here again, one must bear in mind that she used the phone to make numerous and extended toll calls in order to keep in touch with members, to inform them of developments, to seek advice, and to arrange meetings. Over the course of a year, she estimated for us that calls attributable to the network totaled fifteen hundred dollars. When added to lunches, over a two-year period, her total contribution was approximately $3,500.

The reader will recall that, beginning in the third year, it became apparent that the network was growing at a rapid pace and involved such a variety of activities that it was no longer possible for Mrs. Dewar to stay on top of things. A full-time coordinator was necessary, but who should fund the position? There was a prior question, however, that received attention from Mrs. Dewar and Sarason, stimulated by a possibility in the previous year that money could be made available to the network through the county director of manpower, who "happened" to be a network member. Mr. K. had become very intrigued by the barter economy thrust of the network. He had just received federal funds to hire and to train unemployed people, but he wanted to avoid obsolescent "busy work" or dead-end jobs. He wanted to hire people for positions that would give them new skills in new types of positions so that when public monies ceased, as he knew they would someday, these people would stand a good chance of continued employment. If, somehow, the skills these people now possessed could be utilized in or refocused to be relevant to new settings, that would be the most desirable route to go. That way of thinking had been stimulated by discussion in several general meetings about how the schools could use the community for its educational purposes, and also how empty classrooms (and there would be more of them) could be used to serve the educational needs of the adult population, as well as needs for more day-care facilities and personnel. Spontaneously, he raised the possibility of making funds available to the network to help him set up similar networks elsewhere in this large county, as well as to develop network programs for some of the people he would be hiring. The first problem was how to give money to something having no legal status or formal organization. Conceivably, this could be done by assigning the money to a recognized community agency that would be willing to be a conduit between the county and the network. The second problem was: Even if such an arrangement could be set up, did it fit federal regulations? As it turned out, the plan was not feasible on several administrative and legal grounds, an outcome that crystallized only after weeks of effort by Mrs. Dewar and Mr. K.

Sarason had been opposed to the plan. His arguments were several. First, the network was a voluntary, informal association of people not tied or responsible to any external agency. Members could opt in or out at their discretion. If the network assumed the contemplated responsibility, its character would inevitably change, focusing its energies too narrowly, thereby closing off other unexamined options.

Second, how would such a decision be made? Between Mrs. Dewar, Mr. K., and someone from the community agency? If it was a network decision, who was in the network, and by what as yet to be developed rules would they make a decision? The network had no constitution or articulated rules of procedure, but these would have to be formulated if funding was secured. Was the trade-off that obvious in favor of the contemplated funding? Sarason thought not.

Third, public funding is for one year, and in the middle of the first year one has to start worrying about funding for the second year, because one has responsibilities to those one has hired and to the projects under way. Anyone who has had experience with one-year grants, particularly those coming from the public sector, know well the dynamics of which one becomes a prisoner: starting dates; federal, state, or local criteria for hiring and report writing; the pressure to act because one has to demonstrate that one is doing what one said one would do even though the realities of action were not what one anticipated.

The dynamics of grant getting and grant spending in our society have hardly been studied, but to the uninitiated, it can be summed up as a process unwittingly calculated to have the tail wag the dog. The contemplated funding and its mechanism seemed to put very few restrictions on the network, but, as someone once put it, "Famous last words uttered on a road strewn with disillusioned grant getters." Sarason was quite aware of the network's need for a full-time coordinator. The growth of the network was no longer solely due to Mrs. Dewar's energies and imaginativeness. People contacted the network and sought information about it. Indeed, Sarason would get overwhelmed when he thought about what was, would be, and could be going on. How could one limit growth without adverse consequences? The need for a full-time coordinator was, so to speak, a very mixed blessing. On the one hand, it testified to the network's growth; on the other hand, to get a full-time coordinator required money, and getting it without adversely affecting the network would be no easy matter.

Mrs. Dewar was a woman of means and she was prepared to pay for the coordinator. Her reluctance had nothing to do with means or motivation but was based on the belief that any organization serving the community well, and capable of demonstrating that, should be able to find community support to keep it going. This is an understandable position, but certain of its assumptions need explication. For one thing, the position assumes that one is talking about formally organized, legally based organizations having well-formulated, relatively focused missions definable both by type of service and constituency. The Essex network does not possess these characteristics. Furthermore, it assumes that when these organizations receive monies from the community (for example, United Way, public agencies, foundations) because they have demonstrated their value, there are no adverse consequences to being in a dependent relationship. The adverse consequences can run the gamut from a little to an insidiously subversive degree. Sarason's point was that the Essex network would be particularly vulnerable to adverse consequences if the source of funding required that most of its energies go into certain activities. In previous chapters, we have stressed the unpredictable nature and course of network activities, an important factor, we believe, in the degree of interest the network has for its members. To restrict its scope is to make the network more predictable, a more conventional experience for its members.

Sources of funding (particularly public ones) are not noted for their willingness to accommodate to the peculiar needs of grant applicants. On the contrary, grant applicants are too frequently too ready to bend to what they perceive to be the funding agency's desires. But, it could be argued, we live in the real world and we need money to live, and the network is no exception. And would not the network pay a price for remaining "chaste and pure"? Sarason's position was that of course one pays a price, but that is the point: There is always a trade-off and, unfortunately, the possibility of getting funds is a potential trap, because it facilitates glossing over the nature and extent of the trade-off.

These issues became moot when Mr. K. could find no basis in the legislation to fund the network. Unhesitatingly, Mrs. Dewar provided the funds to secure a full-time coordinator. This meant that in the third year of the network she was contributing approximately $20,000: the coordinator's salary and fringe benefits, lunches, and telephone costs. Over the three years, her total contribution was somewhat less than $25,000.

The factors that made it necessary to hire a full-time coordinator have by no means "gone away." Indeed, during this third year, the potential and actual interconnections within the Essex network, and between the network and other individuals, programs, and agencies, are somewhat mind boggling. Even with Mrs. Dewar's undiminished participation and the coordinator's full-time immersion in network activities, we could already foresee the same pressures building up that led to the hiring of the coordinator. The nature of the network generates growth, that is, interconnections and opportunities for resource exchange. Take, for example, the following, which happened at the very end of the third year. Although the principal of the local high school was both supportive of and gratified by the network's role in helping develop programs for his students and faculty, the coordinator was aware of an ambivalence in the principal to the network of which he was long an active participant.[1] Sarason had also sensed the ambivalence, and he was also aware that neither Mrs. Dewar nor the coordinator was dealing with it directly, and that this could well be an important error of omission. If one takes the sense of community seriously, one does not avoid disagreements. At the least, the nature of disagreements has to be clarified. In any event, Sarason and the coordinator met with the principal. Several very surprising facts emerged. First, although the geographical area served by the high school has the appearance of uniform affluence, in fact, it has pockets of poverty as well as those containing working class families. This was not news to us, but what we were not prepared for was the fact that slightly more than half of the graduating class went on to college, far less than we or anybody else in the network would have guessed. The second thing we learned was how alone the principal felt in his effort to develop new programs to better prepare the noncollege-bound student for a productive working life. Furthermore, he said, some of these students should be going on to college. It was a very long conversation, because we started to discuss the different ways the community could be involved in and take some responsibility for locating challenging work-study sites; how one could help teachers in regard to matching student to site; the problems one will encounter to program, curriculum, and logistical changes within the school, as well as the problems that come up in any effort to forge bonds between school and community; how to organize within and without the school a supportive constituency so that the changes would not be seen as the principal's idiosyncratic effort at change; and the different ways in which different members of the network would see it in their interests to be helpful.[2] What the principal had

[1] We do not wish to convey the impression that the network was in some platonic way "responsible" for all the activities in which its members participated. In the case of the local high school, the network's role, except in the case of the university–high-school research project described in Chapter Three, was to help the school to obtain resources it needed for its educational purposes. If the network bears responsibility for anything, it is the dissemination of the idea that there are innumerable ways of exchanging resources in mutually rewarding ways.

[2] An intriguing idea was how to determine the relatively high level of technical skills possessed by some students who then could teach them to other students. For example, some students were sophisticated in electrical

in mind was no small affair, and if he pursued his ideas it would require a discernible portion of the coordinator's time. By the end of his first year, the coordinator felt he had more than he could handle, and in the next year time would become for him an even more precious commodity.

We knew that growth would present problems: financial, conceptual, structural. What we did not and could not know was when the problems would arise, the particular form they would take, and the universe of alternatives available to us for "solutions." We now know there are no solutions in the once-and-for-all sense, but rather that we will always be dealing with the consequences of "problem creation through problem solution," and opportunities seized create new opportunities.

And How Shall the Network Be Judged?

Twenty-five thousand dollars over a three-year period. Was it a complete waste of money? A completely successful venture? Or the usual inbetween? The questions have to be rephrased in terms of the network's different, albeit related, purposes. One must start, however, with a question correlated initially to costs, because if the question can be answered affirmatively, the implications are so sweeping for traditional thinking, practice, and public policy as to dwarf the economic question by one about how do we wish to live? The question is (and was from the beginning): Could we demonstrate that diverse people from diverse agencies and institutions could exchange resources in mutually beneficial ways, without an exchange of funds, and that the vehicle helping to bring this about could be voluntarily sustained and enlarged? Put in another way: Could we bring about sustained resource exchange among individuals from agencies and institutions ordinarily unrelated, or not in contact with, or unknown to each other but who need or can use each other to further their objectives? (By "ordinarily," we mean that in our

---

gadgetry—that is, its functions and repair. Why could they not help other students gain such knowledge and skill? Precisely because half of the student body came from affluent homes, one could assume that among them would be some with very special competencies. But on what basis do we assume that among the less affluent there are not some who possess knowledge and skills they could and should make available to others?

society resource exchange is perceived as requiring money, that is, one *purchases* what one needs, with the consequence that if one does not have money, needs remain unfulfilled.) It is hard to overestimate how different the thrust of the question is from usual thinking and practice and, therefore, how difficult it can be to change what in our society is a highly overlearned way of thinking. Therefore, when we started, our concern was: Could we bring about, to some degree at least, a change that would not dissipate once a resource exchange had occurred? If we could demonstrate that this was possible, it obviously would have enormous implications for how we learn to locate and use resources. We have, to the satisfaction of many people directly and indirectly part of the network, answered the question in the affirmative.

But what if Mrs. Dewar's contribution had not been $25,000 but one million dollars? "Big deal," would be the retort, "with that kind of money your demonstration loses all or most of its significances." The fact is, scores of millions of dollars were spent by the federal government for purposes similar to those of the Essex network, with predictably poor results in any community. The significance of the Essex network is not in its costs, were they small or large, but in the fact that it was started and is voluntarily sustained in ways consistent with its purposes. For example, the import of the activities we described in earlier chapters is not in the fact that there was no money exchange, but rather in the ways a mix of independent individuals and agencies joined in mutually helpful efforts and wish to continue to do so. In regard to each of those activities, we could describe similar efforts around the country that were initiated *after* receiving some kind of grant, usually for more than $25,000 for one year. And we could also describe how the effort usually disappeared or dissipated after the grant period ended.

We do not wish to convey the impression either that the Essex network has been developed in exemplary fashion, or that it took advantage of all the opportunities it could or should have, or that each opportunity that was pursued had clearly successful outcomes. More activities than can be described in this book have had consequences consistent with the rationale, albeit in varying degrees. Indeed, as we stressed in earlier chapters, describing any one of these activities in comprehensive detail is no easy matter and would overwhelm the reader. Furthermore, no one of these activities either in terms of people, discussion, or planning, was unrelated (or stayed unrelated) to other ongoing activities. Therefore, if one tried to determine how much network time (and, consequently, what proportion of the $25,000) went into any one activity, the answer might be clearly quantitative but misleading.

Mrs. Dewar contributed $25,000, not a million, over a three-year period. By usual standards of grant-giving agencies, that is a piddling amount of money, but it was sufficient to bring and sustain in working relationship to each other several score of people from at least a score of colleges, universities, and community agencies.[3]

The network's rationale for resource exchange had nothing to do either with the virtues of frugality and saving money or enchantment with the empty rhetoric of advocates of cost-benefit analyses. Obviously, we are not opposed to frugality and efficiency. What powered our concern was the inability of people to confront squarely the fact of limited resources, but if that was the extent of our concern, we would be in the same camp as those to whom a balanced budget, better yet a reduced one, is the supreme hallmark of human accomplishment. For us, the fact of limited resources presented two types of "opportunities": to seek ways whereby people (including us) could enlarge their knowledge as well as the scope of their interests and talents, and to do this through a quality of human relationship that strengthened a sense of community, the desire for reciprocity, or, at the very least, diluted the strength of the debilitating feeling that one was alone in the world. How does one enhance the self and the satisfactions from human relationships at the same time? How can we take advantage of what we can do rather than passively bemoaning what we cannot do? How do we break out of the isolation forced on us by the barriers between community agencies?

The Essex network has to be evaluated not only in terms of numbers of individuals and agencies, or the outcomes of its differ-

---

[3] If one computed the "salary time" required for the network's resource exchanges, it would be somewhat astronomical and, of course, unobtainable. It was achievable only because the exchanges greatly facilitated accomplishment of "salaried objectives."

ent activities, but also in terms of what it did to people's sense of belonging, further diversification of their interests and talents, and new ways of thinking about resources. These criteria are capable of being evaluated, for example, by interviews with members by "dispassionate individuals," analyses of tapes of meetings. Such data are not available, although we do have some relevant but non-systematic data. We have the spontaneous comments of numerous visitors to meetings, attendance figures for meetings, unsolicited reports by network members, some focused interviews by the coordinator with some network members, requests to join the network, inquiries about its purposes and functioning, and a report on the network requested and done by a representative of a federal agency interested in networks.[4] Undoubtedly, our positive evaluation of our experiences is affected by our inevitable partisanship, but we have endeavored in this book to correct for such bias as much as we consciously could.

There is a final question: When should a network be evaluated? We have endeavored to sketch the development of the Essex network over its first three years. When we took stock after the first year, the most accurate description would have been "ideas in search of opportunities for implementation." At the end of the second year, the opportunities had been found, the ideas began to change and coalesce into a rationale, sources of problems identified, and the dilemmas of growth became apparent. By the end of the third year, a number of network-generated or network-related activities had been launched or successfully carried out, and there was much greater personal and conceptual security about what we were doing, why, and the changes in emphasis that would be required if we were to be more consistent with the network's rationale. We have learned a great deal, and it may well be that what we have learned will turn out to be more important than what we have done, as judged by traditional criteria of accomplishment. The production

---

[4] This was done by Allen Parker for the National Institute of Education. His report, based primarily on many hours of discussion with Mrs. Dewar, lists and describes many of the network's activities ongoing at the beginning of the third year. The network's rationale is very briefly stated and no one activity is described in detail. It is a positive report, and we are indebted to Parker for urging us to write up our experiences in a more comprehensive manner.

ethic is strong in all of us, so that if the gross national product increases, or a public agency or private company spends more money, or if we build more highways, we tend to see these as "progress." Not surprising, because we are part of this culture, there has been the tendency to enthuse over the growth of the Essex network as we have seen the number of participants increase and interconnections forged with other types of networks near and far. In fact, the opportunities for growth are staggering, and we have become aware that this may well be a mixed blessing. The Essex network is at a crucial point, and evaluating it after the next three years will undoubtedly shed light on how we currently judge the first three years. We are not being ritualistically modest and cautious. At the end of the third year, a number of network members are raising questions about "Where have we been and where are we or should we be going?" and these are questions that will be central in future meetings. What is the relationship of all this to finances? The answer has two parts. First, these questions can be raised and discussed because the members realistically perceive that they are not bound by any requirement to produce something in a given period of time, that is, there is no contract among members, or between members and some external source of funds, that says that by a certain date certain things will have been accomplished. If these pressures exist, they are internally generated by the needs, imagination, and enthusiasm of the members. The second part of the answer, of course, is that in her financial support of the network Mrs. Dewar laid down no restrictions whatsoever. And with mention again of Mrs. Dewar, we can no longer postpone confronting a question that has undoubtedly been in the readers' minds: How atypical were the conditions facilitating the development of the Essex network? If we have demonstrated that under unusual conditions one can obtain unusual results, the demonstration may be very interesting but of no general significance or applicability.

Atypical Facilitating Conditions

Mrs. Dewar is an affluent woman with perceived status and influence in the community. Because of her activities on numerous committees and agencies (a long tradition in her family) she knows and has access to professional and business leaders. There is no doubt that when she wishes to bring people together, she can arrange it. So when, in the early days of the network, she wished to bring people together, this was no particular problem. This is not to say that people came simply because she asked them. She did give them reasons that seemed relevant to their purposes. The fact that it was Mrs. Dewar who was asking was not irrelevant, but neither was it a necessary and sufficient condition. Nor can one avoid noting that the possibility of getting to know and work with Mrs. Dewar carries with it another possibility: Perhaps she will find what you are doing sufficiently interesting and important to merit her financial support. And there was and is no one in the Essex network who needed a fraction of a second to figure out how they could use new funds to carry out their programs.

These characteristics and perceptions of Mrs. Dewar undoubtedly explain in part why people came to the early network meetings, but they do not explain why they continued to come over a rather long period of time, involving themselves in ways we have described. As we have stressed, money was never discussed as a requirement for the network's existence, and it was infrequently discussed as a need by the smaller groups organized around a particular activity. If her affluence was initially a factor, it early lost whatever role it was playing.

In raising the question about the degree of atypicality of the origins of the Essex network, it was implied that the factors associated with Mrs. Dewar were all positive and facilitating. This was not the case. For one thing, she had no professional credentials, she was calling together a heterogeneous collection of professionals, and it is no secret that, as a group, professionals do not wax enthusiastic about lay men or women who seem to be taking a leadership role. And, let us not forget, in bringing them together she was tactfully and sensitively presenting ideas about what might and should be but was not being done. Implicitly, she was suggesting that they might consider new ways of thinking. On the surface, at least, the participants listened and reacted positively, but several people later said that they had marked ambivalence about her role. In some of her forays to establish interconnections, Mrs. Dewar met with a mixture of disdain and gruffness. At a general meeting, it had been agreed, as a logical extension of environmental studies, to seek participation by people dealing with systems of protection both for and from the environment. In typical style, she concluded that these were issues that could be addressed by students in a school of public health. Could she find a school that would view such a field experience as potentially enriching to its students? They would be dealing with a "real life" problem, with the opportunity to do something about it. This would require, of course, that some faculty members give some of their time, although sustained supervisory help would be given by appropriate professionals in Essex. So, she arranged to meet with three faculty members from a very prestigious school of public health. It was an embarrassingly unsuccessful meeting. She was treated as an intrusive, ignorant nonentity. When she told Sarason about the meeting, she reported that one of the faculty members seemed interested, but after a time he said relatively little, letting his two colleagues dominate the discussion. A month later, this faculty member called Sarason on a matter utterly unrelated to networks or Mrs. Dewar. Before concluding the phone call, Sarason asked him how the meeting with Mrs. Dewar had gone. In paraphrase, the faculty member said: "I was so embarrassed, I cringed and shut up. Considering how she was treated, Mrs. Dewar bore up rather well. I really thought she was trying to say something important, and I thought we were kindred souls, but I could not wait for the meeting to be over." Sarason told him she had sensed his interest, and he asked this faculty member if he could relay the contents of this telephone discussion to her. To make a long story short, the linkage was reestablished, a public health student was found and is carrying out a project, and there is every expectation that in the future more students will be working with network members.

This was an extreme example, but it does make the point that Mrs. Dewar's lack of professional credentials was by no means a facilitating factor in the early days of the network. Still another factor not in her favor was her lack of experience in running meetings. There are many people who never learn how to run a meeting; Mrs. Dewar was not only aware of her inexperience but also of the fact that network meetings had no rules, attendance was voluntary, participants had diverse interests and goals, and a sense of common purpose would not be easily achieved. Her anxiety level in preparing for and running the early meetings was high and this at times rendered her insensitive to some of the dynamics of the meetings. She did depend considerably on Sarason in preparing for the early meetings and his presence at them was helpful. She learned. The point is that in her case one can too easily attribute the development of the network to her community status and the implicit power stemming from her affluence, neglecting in such a judgment that she had obstacles to overcome because she was perceived as being inexperienced and lacking in professional credentials (although the truth is that she has had more diverse experiences, held more responsible positions, and had in the most self-aware way acquired a depth and scope of knowledge about more fields than most professionals).

To start an Essex-type network requires a person who is perceived as important in some way, who is known to many people, and who has persistence. We do not regard affluence as a necessary characteristic, because we have known many individuals in poverty areas who organized and galvanized people to direct their energies to a particular issue or course of action. Nor do we claim that the Essex-type network is unique. That is to say, we assume that many such informal networks based on a similar rationale exist, although it is unlikely that very many of them have become so differentiated, far-flung, and sustaining. Precisely because the Essex-type network is informal and unincorporated, it is not visible and does not receive public attention. Therefore, to describe the Essex network as unique would be presumptuous and, if we are correct in this belief, it suggests that the development of that network is far from wholly explained by Mrs. Dewar's affluence and status in the larger community.

If anything was atypical about Mrs. Dewar, it was her commitment to and clarity about ideas, such as resource exchange. It was these ideas that early made for meetings stimulating everyone's imagination. We would contend that it was her ideas, far more than affluence and status, that made the difference between the network's viability and an early demise. How else can one explain why so much began to happen so quickly? It could be argued that it was Mrs. Dewar's "connections" that facilitated network interconnections. There is truth to that, but it should not obscure what should be equally obvious: It was her ideas that determined the use and the purposes of the interconnections. There are a lot of people with a lot of connections, but that does not mean they can bring resources together in the way and on the basis Mrs. Dewar did, and help others learn to do the same.

The reader will recall that the Essex network grew out of meetings between Mrs. Dewar, Don Davies, and Sarason. Davies and Sarason provided a good deal of personal and conceptual support to Mrs. Dewar, but it needs to be emphasized that again it was her ideas and persistence that made these people important to her purposes and helped her convince them that *their* purposes could be achieved. A lot of people know or have access to Davies and Sarason, but it took a citizen with ideas and persistence to gain their time and commitment.

No one factor explains the development of the Essex network, but if we are emphasizing the role of ideas or rationale, it is because their strength and attractiveness make other factors less crucial than they probably were in the Essex network. In any community, there are many people with status and perceived influence and power, but there are very few with ideas that unleash people's imagination, bring them into new relationships with each other, and help them move, however small may be the degree, toward their goals.

Money is not a prerequisite for developing an Essex-type network. Leadership, ideas, information, and independence are crucial. If this type of network grows consistently with its purposes, the point may be reached when a coordinator is necessary, and it well can be a moment of truth, because the source from which one may obtain funds, and the formal obligations such funding may require, can undermine the network. With the best of intentions, the network and the funding source can unwittingly "collude" to defeat the purposes of both. Obviously, we cannot assert that there are no conditions by which funding may have desirable consequences. Our experience with the Essex network is too limited, and our experience over the years with the relation between programs and funding too extensive, to permit us to allow optimism and hope to run roughshod over realities of the past.

8

Leadership and the Character of Networks

$\int u u u u u u u u u u u u u u u v$

In Chapter Two, we described an effort to bring resources into a public school. The purpose of that excerpt was to underline how traditional conceptions and definitions of resources drastically limit a school's capacity to accomplish its goals. In this chapter, we shall present another excerpt that allows us to look from another perspective at the issues surrounding the development of the Essex network.

The principal of a high school serving primarily minority students in a medium-sized city approached one of the authors (Cohen) for advice about evaluating a program to be initiated in the next school year. It was early summer, but the principal, together with some teachers, students, and parents, was hard at work generating ideas about how to change curriculum and organizational structure to meet better the needs of students. This summer activity was made possible by a grant from a local foundation. The problems of this school were many and serious. Of three hundred entering freshmen, at least half would be outright academic failures. Attendance was poor. Levels of academic achievement of entering freshmen were usually far from grade or age level, and a significant portion of these freshmen had reading levels ranging from second to fourth grade. And yet, among knowledgeable people within and without the school, the question was not why this school was as bad as it was, but rather why it was as good as it was. Far from being cynical, despondent, or discouraged, the principal and teachers were noted for their drive, ingenuity, and generally good rapport with students and parents. Each year they came up with new ideas. The fact that the local foundation gave them a grant of $25,000 for the summer to mount new programs was testimony to how the principal and teachers were regarded.

Two major changes were contemplated. The first was a "buddy" system, in which each freshman would be assigned to an upperclassman who would help in orientation to the school, as well as in any other way that seemed possible and appropriate. At the end of the previous school year, a list of buddies was developed, meetings were held with them, and before school would begin in the fall training sessions were planned and staff supervisory responsibilities would be clarified. The second major change involved major alterations in the science, social studies, and reading programs. Introduction of the buddy system and the curriculum changes would require some administrative reorganization and a lot more work and responsibility for everyone.

In his initial discussion with the principal, Cohen concluded that program evaluation was the least of the principal's problems, and said so. More important, Cohen said, was how realistic the summer group was in assessing what would be required in terms of time and supervisory personnel to do justice to the goals of the contemplated changes. Knowing as he did that this school normally had pitifully few resources relative to its problems, Cohen intuited that the summer working group was vastly underestimating what, for example, a viable buddy system required. The principal asked if Cohen would come and discuss these questions with the working group. A meeting two weeks hence was arranged, at which time the working group would have a week or so to concretize their plans. It was a two-hour meeting, but by the end of the first fifteen minutes, one thing was clear: the working group knew that they did not have the resources to do what they had proposed to do, that is, to do it with a semireasonable chance of success. They were more anxious than they were discouraged. In addition to their vast underestimation of what their plans had entailed, they found themselves faced with another possibility: the school system was being forced to retrench, and it was far from certain that some of this summer working group would even be in that school when it opened in the fall. If they had accommodated to the fact that their resources would not increase, they had not entertained the possibility that their available resources might be decreased!

We did not present this anecdote to illustrate unrealistic planning, or to emphasize again the fact of limited resources, or to note the strength of the tendency to assume a stable level of available resources. One of our purposes was about a somewhat more subtle and fateful point: *In all of the planning no one ever questioned the assumption that the contemplated program could only be carried out by paid personnel in the school.* That assumption was never made explicit, but all thinking and action were based on it. When Cohen pointed this out, they agreed with him somewhat sheepishly, because both the principal and teachers were committed to community participation in the schools. They treasured that value, and, in some ways, honored it in practice, but when it came to coping with serious problems, they could only think in conventional ways. They realized, of course, that there were many people in the community who could be helpful to them in moving in new directions, but their stance was that of a hungry, penniless person reading a mouth-watering menu in the restaurant window. How could this working group approach community people for their advice and time if they could not pay them? The answer, of course, is in two parts. First, as members of the community, these people had a responsibility to help the schools. The schools have not and will never have resources to deal adequately, let alone excellently, with the problems of children. Second, we vastly underestimate how community people, professional and lay, long for ways to participate that they consider socially worthwhile and as introducing novelty and challenge into their lives. We do not wish to convey the impression that, if given the opportunity, community people will come flocking to the schools with offers of time and help. But neither do we wish to downplay our experience, and that of others, that when participation in schools is presented and experienced as a mutually rewarding experience—not a ritualistic, one-way give-but-not-get opportunity—significant community resources will become available.

The anecdote allows us to make a point more directly relevant to questions about the Essex network, and it concerns that school principal. He is a forceful, articulate, persistent, and courageous person who has been able to prevent a serious situation from becoming a catastrophic one. Although an overworked word, *charismatic* does apply to him. In addition, he has made it his business to know community people, and he is known by more people than he himself knows. He is part of diverse types of community and professional networks. *If he were able to think of resource exchange the way Mrs. Dewar did, he could develop an Essex-type network.* Indeed, he would have one advantage over Mrs. Dewar at the time she developed the Essex network. This principal has a keen sense of the significance of the sense of community, more than Mrs. Dewar had when she started. When Cohen (at the meeting of the summer work group) briefly discussed the concept of network, this principal immediately grasped how the concept in action could be an antidote to the social forces that separate people from each other. This principal did not have Mrs. Dewar's affluence or perceived status as an influential or powerful person in the community, but he shared other characteristics with her far more crucial than affluence or perceived power. However, he was a prisoner of traditional thinking in that he defined resources as that which a school could pay for and allocate. It was not that the barter type of resource exchange was foreign or bothersome to him; rather, his training, as well as his experience in a system that reinforced traditional ways of thinking, pushed the barter-type way of thinking out of awareness.

What would happen if this principal (or others like him) began to think and act in accordance with the rationale we have described in this book? Some problems are predictable. For example, to develop and sustain an Essex-type network requires time, and part of that time will be spent away from the school. Initially, the principal will feel a tension between what he is doing to develop the network and what he has been taught a principal should be doing and where, especially if the school is beset with problems. And if he can cope with this tension, he is likely to find others in the school system who look disapprovingly on his activities and style. If he brings in community people to perform certain functions that are not being done by school personnel (who would like to perform those functions but who either lack the time or expertise), he can expect resistance. And if he brings in community people who have no professional credentials (Mrs. Dewar), he can count on trouble from different quarters. Good ideas, like love, are necessary but not sufficient to achieve stated goals. Ideas exist in the minds of real people who exist in real organizations, and to judge ideas independent of the culture of the organization in which they are to be applied is unjust to the ideas and to deny what we know about organizational craziness. The Essex network was deliberately kept as a network of individuals, as a way of avoiding the constraints of organizational inertia and inflexibility, as well as a way of quietly planting in organizations the seeds of change, and we never fooled ourselves that the soil would always be fertile. The Essex network was started by someone outside of formal organizations. When such a network is started by someone in an organization and he or she takes responsibility for its nurturance, its course would have to be different than that of the Essex network. The rationales may be similar, if not identical, but applied in different contexts they must be expected to appear different. Concern about "boundaries" between and within organizations is characteristic of formal organizations, and this concern can be a most effective barrier against the purposes of networking. When these boundaries are justified, as they usually are, on the grounds of autonomy, tradition, and efficiency, it is obvious that any network rationale based on a barter economy conception will be held suspect. (And if part of the justification implicitly assumes competition as an unalloyed virtue, the barriers to consideration of the rationale become even stronger.) As always in these matters, at the root is the question of values and their consequences. Consider this in terms of industrial organizations:

> It is my belief that *management with all of its employees* and the *union with all of its members* have an untapped, unlimited potential in the *responsible* man-

agement of *all* their resources or assets: The customer in the national and international marketplace; the employees from the sophisticated technology to the sophisticated assembly and services; the financial resources of capital investors in brick, mortar, equipment, to the hourly rate and extensive fringe benefits, the vendors who develop and service with ingenious and reliable parts.

That mutual responsibility is not possible when a company is addressed as "the enemy," when the vocabulary is exclusively what can we get, what will they give, what is the minimum and what is the maximum demand. The adversarial role is obsolete in 1976 if the leadership of management and the union is going to *serve* the interests of the employees and their membership. Self-service and political ambition in such power positions is the most corrupting influence. The leadership and education of the followers is the only solution which will enable employees to become mature, responsible, involved industrial citizens. The cost of industrial delinquency in absenteeism, turnover, unreliable quality, added-on and excessive costs, and marginal profitability is suicidal bankruptcy for our industrial organizations and our free enterprise system. Our industrial and service organizations are the common responsibilities of management and unions. These organizations are the only means of assuring our free society, advancing technologies, our security, survival, and standard of living. [Frost, 1976, pp. 6–7; italics in original]

Those words, like those of the rationale of the Essex network, sound noble, utopian, and worthy of a place in the file-and-forget cabinet: "*All of its members* have an untapped, unlimited potential in the responsible management of *all* their resources or assets." Those words are, in spirit, identical to aspects of the rationale of the Essex network, especially in regard to the view that a person is not *a* single resource but is a number of resources, and that in releasing these resources a quantitative change can be transformed into a qualitative one. Those words and the values they imply are the basis for "The Scanlon Plan":

The Scanlon Plan is no panacea. It is not for everyone. It is not a substitute for ineffective management. It is no remedy for bellicose, nontrusting industrial relationships. It is not permissive.

It is *not* an incentive system. It is a process of organization development which is based upon the fact that every individual—employee, executive—every organization, is in the state of becoming better or worse, never static. Man is a growing, learning animal and he or she spends a major portion of his or her waking life growing and learning in industrial, institutional, or governmental environments.

Mindful of the fact that McGregor's Theory Y states clearly that human behavior is the *CONSEQUENCE,* not the cause of how man is treated, it seems only rational that the leadership of organizations ought to accept the opportunity and responsibility for its members *learning* the operational facts of life. They should identify that their assets are the marketplace, the physical resources, the financial resources, and the human resources. They should learn to accept the responsibility for the effective management of these assets to assure competitive position, profitability, and an improving return on their lifetime investment in their job assignment. They should learn the consequences of being irresponsible. [Frost, 1976, pp. 7–8]

The Scanlon Plan has been implemented in numerous industrial organizations, and it has attracted a good deal of attention. It is beyond our purposes to judge and evaluate the Scanlon Plan in action, but it is relevant here to paraphrase what Frost told us in an extended interview (October 21, 1976):

We get many requests from companies to help implement the Scanlon Plan, but we follow through in very few instances, because after the first meeting it becomes clear to them and us that they really have not comprehended the basic conceptions of the plan: that by its very nature it is not a process legislated from on high; that it requires a very different way of viewing and

relating to people; that if the potentials of their human
resources are to be realized in a mutually rewarding and
responsible way, people must be provided with and have
access to all relevant information about their working
environment; that the greatest obstacle to truly accepting
the process on the part of most people in the organization
is the invalid idea that self-interest does not ultimately
depend on group interest; that the development of an
individual's potentials is not a symbiotic function of the
same development in those around him; that the
strength of leadership will depend less on the authority
of ownership and more on the formulation of and adher-
ence to an organizational mandate that *begins* the
process through which everyone develops the sense of
"problem ownership"; and, what wraps it all up, that
when a company says that its employees are its most
valued resource, is it willing to take that seriously or will
it continue to be content to view them as mindless, un-
differentiated cogs? So we follow through with very few
companies, even though all of them are hurting, are
admittedly inefficient, caught up in adversarial conflicts,
the heads-I-win, tails-you-lose way of living.

We learned two other things from Frost that are directly
relevant to our discussion of networks. Frost and his colleagues,
based at Michigan State University, receive no personal compensa-
tion for their services. There is no fee for any preliminary discussions
with companies who are not even asked to cover the costs of travel
(which may be to any place in the United States). If there is agreement that minimal conditions exist for the successful implementation
of the plan, a fee is charged that goes to the university and is used
to cover student stipends and travel costs. What this means is that
Frost is unusually free, not only to be forthright, but to keep his
focus on the consistency between rationale and action. As best as
we can gather, and we quizzed Frost rather intensively on this point,
once there is agreement to implement the plan, Frost seems to play a
role remarkably similar to that of Mrs. Dewar in the Essex network.
He has and would take no authority in implementation. He is available to any individual or group in the company, but his primary role

concerns the consistency between action and the agreed-on mandate. He does not represent management. He represents a set of values, conceptions, and process about which there has been agreement, and his obligation is to help everyone translate this agreement to the level of action. He would deny that he is a leader or coordinator, and in a formal sense he is correct, but, like Mrs. Dewar, he seems to be granted a role of influence because of how he thinks and conducts himself, how what he stands for strikes a responsive chord in others, how "the plan" holds out promise for greater meaning and community in life. Frost and Mrs. Dewar never heard of each other, their personalities and styles of action are quite different overtly, their arenas of activity are obviously different, their language is dissimilar (Frost never used the word *network*), and yet both developed not only an amazingly similar conception of resources and their exchange, but came up with a process by which the release of these resources adds a distinctively positive qualitative factor to people's sense of personal productivity and interrelationships. The Scanlon Plan and the rationale of the Essex network do have "technologies," but they are in the service of explicit and agreed-on values, not the least of which is voluntary participation.

9

Understaffed Settings, Values, and Resources

We now take up a concept and body of research that ordinarily would not be included in the literature on networks, because the concept of network does not appear in the titles of publications and the substantive thrust of the research appears very tangential to networks. And yet, the thrust of the research findings are more supportive of the rationale for the Essex network than most of the literature we have reviewed. We refer here to the work of Roger Barker, his colleagues, and others whom he has influenced (for example, Barker, 1968; Barker and Gump, 1964; Wicker, 1973; Wicker and Kirmeyer, 1976). Barker's work has taken place in the framework of an ecological psychology, the dimensions and depth of which are quite impressive, but beyond our present purposes. What is central to our purposes is his discussion of the interplay between people and their environments under different conditions of "manning." Undermanning is the condition

117

of having insufficient or barely sufficient personnel in a setting to carry out the essential tasks and functions. What, Barker asked, are the differences for setting occupants when they are in an under-manned, or adequately manned, or overmanned setting? From the standpoint of the rationale of the Essex network, this question is quite relevant to our discussion of limited resources. The under-manned setting is, by definition, one in which resources are very limited. Barker's research suggests that "in order to maintain the setting under these adverse conditions, the occupants both receive and produce more frequent, stronger, and more varied messages regarding the carrying out of the setting's essential activities than would be the case if the number of persons available were at or above the optimal level" (Wicker and Kirmeyer, 1976, p. 159). Wicker and Kirmeyer summarize the advantages of the under-manned setting suggested by the research as follows.

1. Greater effort to support the setting and its functions, either by "harder" work or by spending longer hours
2. Participation in a greater diversity of tasks and roles
3. Involvement in more difficult and more important tasks
4. More responsibility in the sense that the setting and what others gain from it depend on each individual occupant
5. Viewing oneself and others in terms of task-related characteristics, rather than in terms of social-emotional characteristics
6. Greater functional importance of individuals within the setting
7. Less sensitivity to and less evaluation of differences between people
8. Setting of lower standards and fewer tests for admission into the setting
9. A lower level of maximal or best performance
10. Greater insecurity about the eventual maintenance of the setting
11. More frequent occurrences of success and failure, depending on the outcome of the setting's functions

What is fascinating about this list is the level of the sense of community conveyed and the differentiated, flexible use of available resources. Put in another way, faced with the fact of limited and inadequate resources, the undermanned setting (in contrast to the others) frequently is distinguished by a personal interactional network of relationships based on the need for community and by a discernibly less precious definition of internal and external resources. The linkage between the sense of community and the accommodation to the fact of limited resources is amazingly similar to the rationale for the Essex network. Although this is not an argument to underman settings deliberately, it does raise the thorny question of growth: On what basis does one decide that further growth will subvert the settings' purposes? Indeed, this is the question we confronted as we saw the Essex network extend itself in terms of linkages, projects, and geography. From the standpoint of accommodating to the fact of limited resources, this growth is cause for satisfaction, as are the opportunities provided network members to venture in new directions and to give expression to their different interests and talents. But this growth may adversely affect the sense of community that network members can experience, and if that issue is not satisfactorily resolved, it will be another example of the quantitative submerging the qualitative.

The Essex network is not, in Barker's terms, a behavior setting but, nevertheless, the consequences of growth for network members and occupants of a behavior setting (for example, church, school, post office) can be very similar if among their major purposes are the development and maintenance of a sense of community. There is little in Barker's conceptualizations and writings that speaks directly to the psychological sense of community. Indeed, Barker seems deliberately to avoid discussion of values in his studies of communities from a systematic ecological perspective and methodology. And yet, his concentration on the consequences of the size of membership in a behavior setting on the quantity and quality of interrelatedness strongly suggests that this concentration stems in part from his belief that there are advantages to "smallness" that are undercut by uncritical acceptance of growth as a value. It is not relevant to Barker's ecological purposes to ask how members of an undermanned behavior setting view and would manage an increase in resources. We would predict that far more often than not they would see such growth as an unalloyed "good," unaware that this growth may dilute members' sense of worth and community.

There is an ironic paradox inherent in the rationale of the Essex network, a paradox we have experienced in practice, and that has been a far from muted thread in our discussion. We have argued and demonstrated that the Essex-type network discernibly increases resources available to individuals and, through them, to agencies. Resources are and will always be limited, but if one can unlearn the traditional perception of resources in terms of money, control, and "ownership"—the perception that locks people into circumscribed psychological and "within agency" boundaries—the discrepancy between goals and resources shrinks, at the same time that the sense of community expands and the feeling of personal challenge and growth deepens. Far from being a deficit, the fact of limited resources can be viewed as an opportunity through which to link qualitative and quantitative aspects of social living at work or elsewhere. It is, perhaps, necessary to reiterate that we are not in favor of limited resources and undermanned settings. (That would be like saying that because adversity sometimes forces people to creative and imaginative action, we should in principle be in favor of adversity.) We do maintain that, faced with limited resources, there are partial solutions that can avoid either the poor morale due to the perception of limited or inadequate resources or, in what initially appears to be the best of all possible worlds, the destructive consequences of an increase in traditionally defined resources. The ironic paradox arises in that in the development of an Essex-type network there can be a dramatic increase in available resources (in terms of people), so as to produce the negative features of bigness: reduction in the quantity and quality of face-to-face interactions, constriction in the scope of interests and roles, and a dilution in the awareness of common purposes and origins. That this may occur is not surprising, because the members of an Essex-type network are also members of a larger society that has built into it the confusion between growth and progress. At the same time that we recognize the confusion, we can underestimate the strength of the degree to which we are victims of it.

The development of the Essex network is quintessentially a reflection of the times. World War II and its aftermath not only exposed the degree of interrelatedness among and within societies, but also presented a picture of the future portraying a mind-boggling increase in interrelatedness. At the same time that the world as a total network began to seep into our consciousness, and we began to perceive the fantastic degree of interrelatedness in our own society, we were forced to recognize that the quality of this interrelatedness was characterized by hostility, alienation, loneliness, anomie, aimless drift—the characterizations are many and varied, but all dysphoric. People *knew* they were parts of and enmeshed in myriad networks, but they rarely *felt* a sense of satisfaction or meaningful participation. And to top this cake of personal insignificance and frustration, there was the icing (and it was chilling) of limited and misused resources. We were told and we believed that ours was a society so rich in resources that to solve any major problem required only an act of national resolve. We now know that this is not true for our society or any other. We also know, as never before, that something is "wrong," but we also know that what is wrong is not a *thing* but rather some dimly perceived amalgam of values, definitions, and things; of an ever-increasing tension between pressures for change and the forces of habit and tradition; of a raging struggle between centrifugal and centripetal social forces. In light of all this, it should occasion no surprise that the Essex network should have developed. The Essex network is literally a child of its times.

In one respect, however, the rationale for the Essex network is distinctive, although by no means unique. It is a rationale that has tried to link values and resources, to see the most poignantly felt needs of individuals in relation to a reconceptualization of resources. In our society, we have learned that bigger is not necessarily better, and that the correlation, on the one hand, between increased expenditures to purchase more resources and, on the other hand, intended outcomes is disturbingly low. The reasons for this are many, but surely among the most important is the failure to state clearly the values informing actions and programs, a failure that has two seriously adverse consequences: The significance and difficulty of ordering values in some hierarchical fashion is grossly oversimplified (as if the several values usually involved are equally important), and there is little or no recognition that for any one value there is a universe of alternatives by which it may be given expression. Clarity and agreement on values are crucial first steps, but once they are obtained, one is confronted with "problem creation through problem solution," because there is no one way to act consistent with the values. And when one moves from values to action, particularly in the realm of social problems, one not only finds that the real world is not organized in ways and on bases congenial to one's values, but, no less significant, that one has not paid attention to the implications of these values for how one defines necessary resources. The failure to give attention to the conceptual and practical links between values and resources helps set the stage for disappointments about un-achieved objectives. The rationale for the Essex network attempts to forge these linkages, and to forge and capitalize on these linkages required that we try to demonstrate that once people could under-stand the rationale for them, their ways of utilizing each other would decrease the discrepancy between what they wished to and could do, at the same time that their sense of worth and community would be enlarged and deepened.

The Essex network is a very modest venture, but it has implications, we believe, far beyond its size, circumscribed locale, and accomplishments. Because of its informal and voluntary char-acter, as well as the feature that it is a network of individuals and not of formally and legally constituted organizations, questions can be raised as to the applicability of the rationale within and among such organizations. These are legitimate questions, but they should not obscure the fact that almost invariably network members were part of formal, bureaucratically organized agencies. Nevertheless, the question remains about the feasibility of the rationale for the development of Essex-type networks in such organizations. To pur-sue the question to the world of action requires, of course, a knowl-edge of and commitment to the rationale. We are not indulging in wishful thinking when we say that such knowledge and commitment may increasingly be forthcoming, although we hasten to add that we in no way subscribe to the view that the present is pregnant with the future. The present is pregnant with many futures (for example, Nisbet, 1969). If we allow ourselves to entertain a small fraction of hope, it is based on the fact that with most people in organizations, and at all levels of these organizations, there is festering dissatisfaction with self in work and nonwork roles. And this is no longer true only for moderately educated, nonprofessional workers. It is now true for ever-increasing professional segments of society, as Sarason's (1977) recent book demonstrates. It is a general dissatisfaction at the core of which is a rebellion against narrow work roles, unused talents, unexploited interests, personal isolation in a sea of humanity, and a cult of efficiency that delivered more than it promised by making people servants of technology. The system has triumphed and the individual seems to have lost. If we allow ourselves to hope that the conflict is not quite over, it is because of our experience in the development and maintenance of the Essex network. It may be too frail a reed to grasp to sustain hope, especially because we do not pretend that our rationale is as substantial or as elegant as it might be, or that we were as able as we might have been in implementing it. And yet, when we reflect on what the experience has meant for many of us in the network, how it altered our thinking and practice, we do believe that what we have reported speaks directly to many of the sources of the dissatisfactions in our society.

Our experience with networks is limited. As we shall see in the following pages, a good deal of research has been done on the concept of networks, but only a small part of it has been on action networks based on some explicit rationale. We know the Essex network, but there are few other descriptions of action networks to permit us to make secure generalizations. Between rationale and action is an obstacle course, and if that course is not successfully traversed (or if it is successfully traversed), the single case cannot tell one whether to blame or praise the rationale or the actions. The Essex network is a single case.

10

Meaning and
Distinctiveness of Networks

$\mathcal{U}\mathcal{U}\mathcal{U}\mathcal{U}\mathcal{U}\mathcal{U}\mathcal{U}\mathcal{U}\mathcal{U}\mathcal{U}\mathcal{U}\mathcal{U}\mathcal{U}$

Certain aspects of the literature on networks illuminate particular workings of the Essex network, and at times provide a broader context for understanding it. This literature speaks to a basic concern, in that it conveys a fairly comprehensive sense of the complex interrelationships among constituent elements of modern communities. Sarason (1976a) has suggested that efforts at community and social change up to this time have succeeded poorly because the interveners typically lacked an adequate understanding of the interrelatedness characteristic of contemporary communities.

In a larger sense, this review is an attempt to contribute to a conceptual base for a better understanding of community interrelatedness and strategies for social action and change. The concept that will be developed is that of network. There are many concepts other than networks that social scientists have utilized to understand interrelatedness, including system, informal relations, intergroup relations, and kinship. Although these concepts are extremely important, network concepts open to view essential aspects of interrelatedness that these more widely known concepts fail to capture. In fact, the understanding of society obtained through the lens of the network concept is distinctively different from the view given by these more traditional concepts. Hopefully, a changed perspective on the nature of society will lead to changed conceptions of the nature, process, and problems of efforts of change within modern communities.

This review will cover many academic disciplines. Network concepts have developed in more than a dozen fields, including sociology, anthropology, psychiatry, psychology, administrative sciences, geography, city planning, communications engineering, and several different subfields within these disciplines. The physical science and applied technical fields generally focus on electrical, mathematical, communication and transportation networks, while the social science disciplines most often are concerned with networks among individuals or organizations. Although there need be no relationship among the usages of the same term in different fields, in this case the general attributes of the term network are remarkably consistent across fields. This is especially noteworthy, since individuals using network concepts in any one field often are unaware of the concept's use in other fields; there is little if any cross-indexing among fields. The fact that similar network concepts arose independently in a large number of fields suggests that network is a needed and potentially powerful concept of describing and providing insights into many aspects of contemporary society.

In Chapter Two, we briefly outlined a number of different emphases of meanings applied to the word *network*. While these differences are important, in this part of the review we emphasize instead the commonalities underlying the development and usage of network concepts in various fields. Two important commonalities are: (1) the recognition that various aspects of societal life and functioning are increasingly becoming complexly interrelated; and (2) the belief that the development of conceptualizations and descriptive analyses based on the basic structural interrelationships (networks) among individuals or organizations can provide distinctive insight into contemporary interrelatedness.

In this chapter of the review, the meaning and distinctiveness of the concept of network is briefly explained. Then we draw on network literature to demonstrate the advantages obtained when network concepts are utilized in analyzing four important domains of societal life: the interpersonal, interorganizational, intraorganizational, and public sector decision-making realms. The amount of literature reviewed within each domain is kept to a minimum so that the reader unfamiliar with the fields will not be overburdened with information. Nonetheless, the reader should realize that there may be difficulty integrating the information from one domain to the next, and thus, after these four domains, we try to integrate the information and reemphasize the major point: that networks provide a particular world view that is a useful contribution to our understanding of many aspects of contemporary communities. Chapter Ten concludes with a brief discussion of the historical context out of which network study arose.

Chapter Eleven includes reviews of network literatures that are directly relevant for social change efforts. First, several social science subfields in which the concept of network is used to understand naturally occurring processes related to individual and community change are covered. Then literature in which network conceptualizations are used to understand or propose actual strategies for change is reviewed.

In order to define a discrete structure for study, most social scientists have focused on the linkages and/or interactions of one individual, family, or organization with other such units.[1] The focal unit is often termed the *ego*. All other units of the same type (individuals, families, or organizations) that have direct and indirect linkages and/or interactions with the ego are considered part of that ego's network. This network structure is often conveyed by an image of concentric circles surrounding the ego. Within the first circle are all those units having direct ties with the ego. Within the second circle are all those units having direct ties with the units in

---

[1] Some organizational network analysts have focused on "mesh networks," which are not centered on any single organization.

the first circle, but not having direct ties with the ego. A third, fourth, and fifth circle, and so on, can be described. These circles have often been termed *zones;* for example, the primary zone, secondary zone, and so on. Although this unlimited structure is conceptualized, few social or organizational network analysts have studied this "total" network. Rather, many scientists focus their study on a part (termed the partial network) of the total network that serves a particular function for the individual or organization, for example, getting an individual elected to public office. Others limit their research to those individuals, families, or organizations who interact directly with the focal unit. Thus, each analyst may define his network for study somewhat differently from others; at the same time, the image of an ego surrounded by concentric circles of other units is held in mind by almost everyone.

Before plunging into the review, it would further help the reader to understand some attributes of networks that make them distinct from other ways of looking at interactions, for example, through system and group concepts. There are three distinctive attributes that will be discussed: (1) every unit in a network does not interact with every other unit in a network; (2) the units in a single network do not have a clear boundary from the rest of the world; and (3) the only common characteristic of units in a network is their relationship (direct or indirect) to the ego.

First, the individuals, families, or organizations that are part of an ego's network do not necessarily have interrelationships with each other. Both group and system conceptualizations, in contrast, specify that the component units have interdependent roles related to the functioning of the group or system as a whole. Network formulations may more accurately reflect the actual experiences of individuals, families, or organizations within their environment. The number of actual linkages among units in a specified zone of a network, as compared with the total possible number of such linkages, is known as the *density* of the network. Networks can be compared as to their relative densities. For example, if many of an individual's friends are also friends of each other, then that person has a high-density network; if another individual's friends generally do not know each other, then that individual has a low-density network. As we shall see later, the density of individual, family, and organizational networks in a community has been shown to have major implications for individual, family, organizational, and community functioning and change.

Second, a network is not surrounded by a clear boundary. Rather, a network extends far out in numerous directions into the environment through indirect ties and can never be fully described and a boundary drawn.[2] Many social scientists do limit the part of the total network they consider but, even so, a clear boundary is hard to specify, since networks are always changing as the focal unit develops relationships with new units. Groups and systems, on the other hand, are both defined in part through specification of their boundaries.

Third, the only characteristic that all members of a network have in common is their relationship (direct or indirect) to the ego. The members of a network do not necessarily share common aims, a distinctive subculture, or other traditional social science categorical features generally attributed to both groups and systems. Whereas group and system conceptualizations are employed to simplify the complexity of societal phenomena by clustering individuals according to distinguishing social characteristics, and organizations according to distinguishing functional characteristics, network concepts allow the description of the actual complexity of societal phenomena. This complexity includes the reality that important direct and indirect interactions on a large scale occur between focal individuals or families and social-categorically diverse individuals or families, and between focal organizations and

[2] This was a point we stressed in our attempt to describe the development and scope of the Essex network. In the early phase of that network, the problem of description and boundaries centered on Mrs. Dewar and the relationship of network members to her. She was, so to speak, the ego. However, as the network grew, direct interactions with Mrs. Dewar became proportionately less as direct linkages among members increased. The Essex network was (relatively speaking) a dense one in the sense that everyone knew and had a linkage to Mrs. Dewar and with each other, whereas initially everyone had a direct linkage to her. Although this development is normal or usual, it presented a special problem for the Essex network because of the importance that network's rationale placed on a sense of community and of common origins and purposes. What in a statistical sense is normal or usual was, for the Essex network, not to be confused with what was desirable.

functionally diverse organizations. For example, the concept of a mental health system generally indicates that the organizations that are important in the provision of mental health services include all those organizations that function as direct providers of mental health services in a specified geographical area. The delineation of the total network of a mental health organization, on the other hand, would probably indicate that the delivery of mental health services depends on interactions with mental health, business, political, community, governmental, media, and diverse human service organizations. A social network conceptualization more accurately reflects the reality of the complexity of organizational interactions. Other examples of this idea and the other general ideas presented here will be apparent in the review that follows.

Interpersonal Relationships

Interpersonal relationships and contacts represent a major means through which individuals exert an impact on their environment (for example, achieve personal goals) and through which the environment influences individuals (for example, transmits norms and values). In the stereotypical isolated and relatively stable rural village of the past, the important community with whom an individual interrelated in his or her lifetime was limited to a relatively small, stable group of persons. Each of these individuals might simultaneously be friend, coworker, neighbor, and/or kin to each other and meet a diverse array of each other's emotional, economic, and social needs. Outside of this small group, each individual presumably also had important, although less intensive, contact with other members of the village, but with few persons outside of the localized setting. The "personal community" (Henry, 1958) of the stereotypical rural villager—that is, those individuals who constitute a person's consequential interpersonal world—was tightly bounded, including only a limited number of direct relationships with individuals who were relatively homogeneous in type and often well known to each other.

The geographic, time, and psychological/attitudinal boundaries that insulated the village and personal communities of the past began "breaking open" as the rural society became an increasingly urban one. The development of rapid transportation and communication networks played a crucial role in this change, as did the general societal forces of industrialization, urbanization, rapidly expanding population growth, industrial/occupational specialization, and social mobility. As a result, the personal communities of individuals living in contemporary society, rural or otherwise, are vastly different than ever before, and they are still changing. As Craven and Wellman (1973) point out, in contemporary society individuals are likely to come into contact and need to deal with large numbers of diverse individuals many of whom affect to varying extents the life of the individual. Most of these individuals will not know each other. And since each of these individuals interacts with and is affected by a large number of diverse other individuals (and so on), the life of any one individual is affected by a large number of diverse indirect, as well as direct, relationships. In direct contrast to life in the stereotypical rural village, in contemporary urban life different individuals are likely to be kin, friends, coworkers, and neighbors to each other, and a diverse number of different relationships are likely to be utilized to meet different individual, economic, social, job-related, recreational, and informational needs. In addition, social and geographic mobility and changing personal needs and goals ensure that new direct and indirect relationships and contacts will be forming over time, and old ones falling into disuse. In short, the worlds of contemporary individuals are likely to be composed of a large number of diverse individuals, most of whom will not know each other, and to be changing in composition as new direct and indirect relationships evolve over time.

It is the belief of Craven and Wellman (1973), and of increasing numbers of social scientists, that the concept most useful in studying and understanding the complex reality of the contemporary interpersonal world is that of social network. A social network is generally centered around a particular person (called the *ego*) and, broadly defined, includes all those persons known by the ego who also know him/her and all those individuals with whom the ego has an indirect (that is, potential) relationship. In order to study social networks, researchers have adapted a number of methodological and mathematical techniques to analyze the differential relationships connecting the ego and the various members of the network. These "network analysis" techniques range from simple representations of a limited number of network linkages, in the form of simple graphs or matrices, to sophisticated mathematical and computerized techniques (for example, smallest-space analysis) that are capable of portraying in graphic form the structure of the interrelationships among very large numbers of individuals in a network.[3] The exact conceptual, data collection, and analytical means utilized to study social networks have varied from study to study. The unifying link among most fields concerned with "network analysis," be these in the physical, applied, or social sciences, is topological graph theory. Hebert and Murphy (1970) divide graph-based network analysis into five areas of research: (1) physical structure (relationship between nodes and arcs); (2) flows (maximizing flows from one node to another using the entire network); (3) random graphs (total number of possible graphs of the system); (4) design (to derive optimal networks); and (5) routing (to navigate optimally through the network).

The uses of social network conceptualizations and analyses have expanded rapidly since Barnes' (1954) pioneer work, described hereafter, and now constitute a major mode and area of research in sociology and social anthropology. These researchers have utilized social networks to study numerous, diverse types of issues and problems in contemporary societal life. In the remainder of this section, we do not attempt to review this rapidly growing and diverse literature. Rather, we draw on a limited number of studies to demonstrate the potential distinctiveness and fullness of vision achieved when the social world is viewed through the lens of social network concepts and analyses.

One major advantage of social network conceptualizations is that they are centered on the behavior of specific individuals

---

[3] In describing the Essex network, we deliberately eschewed use of complicated graphic means of presentation, and for one major reason. What is distinctive about the Essex network is not its actual and potential complexity (growth in the number of direct and indirect linkages, geographical spread, and alterations in the centrality of certain individuals), but its rationale and problems of implementation. It is our belief that these mathematically based graphic techniques will gain explanatory power when they are applied to several networks having similar rationales, permitting "within type" as well as "between type" analyses.

(that is, the network's ego) and thus allow the social scientist to focus on the influence that individuals have on the interpersonal environment around them. The individual is conceived of as active and exerting considerable influence on his social network, rather than conceived of as the passive recipient of environmental influence as in the work of many sociologists. Mitchell (1969) claims that network analysis puts the individual back at the center of sociology, as Durkheim originally had done.[4] Social scientists have utilized network conceptualizations and analyses to study, for instance, the active use of social networks by individuals in getting a job (Granovetter, 1970), achieving social mobility (Thompson, 1973), migrating to new locations (Tilly and Brown, 1967), and acquiring needed social services (Lee, 1969).

Lee's (1969) study of how abortionists were located is an example of a study in which network analysis illuminates the use of interpersonal resources in the achievement of personal goals. The study, performed at a time when abortion services were not publicly available, as they are now, revealed that abortion seekers often tried many unproductive contacts before a productive one was finally found, and that the ultimately successful "path" to the discovery of an abortionist varied among individuals from one to seven "links." Although the first contacts made were usually with intimate friends, the pressure to find an abortionist within the limited time during which the abortion was possible forced many individuals to make their first contact with someone whom they did not know very well, but whom they believed would have the necessary information or know someone who might. Lee found that those individuals who have relatively large networks, in which many members do not know each other but have many connections outside the "primary zone," were most likely to succeed in finding an abortionist. Other

---

[4] Mitchell's claim, of course, is well illustrated in the Essex network. Although Mrs. Dewar is the clearest example of how an individual exerts an active and considerable influence on his or her social network, there were many other individuals who, as a result of being in the Essex network, began to assume a more active stance in regard to influencing their environment. One of the potentially exciting consequences of network conceptualizations is that at the same time that they bring the individual to center stage, they permit us to focus on the combined effects of ideas and social interrelationships on the individual, that is, they require us to see the person in terms of interpersonal and cognitive linkages and exchanges.

researchers have similarly found that such far-reaching, "loose-knit" networks generally are most likely to help individuals to acquire tangible resources (Craven and Wellman, 1973).

Network conceptualizations are equally important in understanding how the environment exerts an influence on individuals. An important advantage of network studies in this regard is that they force the researcher to consider the influence of different types of direct and indirect network ties on the behavior of individuals. The differential importance of "weak" (that is, nonintense acquaintance) and "strong" interpersonal ties, for instance, are exemplified in Epstein's (1961) study of the transmission of norms in a single social network. Epstein first mapped out the social network of a single resident in a rapidly growing urban area in Africa. Within this network, Epstein distinguished between the effective part of the network, that is, the part where most people in the individual's network also knew each other, and the extended part that included people who did not know each other and with whom the ego had weaker ties (for example, people of higher social status and people from other towns). Epstein found that the effective network played a major role in social control through the discussions and gossip that it carried. This talk tended to reaffirm behavioral and social norms already held in common by the effective network. On the other hand, he found that new norms tended to rise within the effective network of highly prestigious people in the community and then to filter down to others through extended networks, thus providing a stimulus for norm change.

Another important way in which network conceptualizations open up new avenues of research in studying the effect of the interpersonal environment on individuals is consideration of the influence of different types of network structures on the behavior of individuals. Laumann (1973), for instance, in his Detroit area study found that individuals in "interlocking" social networks (that is, close-knit networks in which the best friends of the ego are also best friends of each other) were more likely to have stable, highly committed opinions and attitudes compared to individuals in "radial" social networks in which their friends are not friends of each other. Bott (1957), in an influential study that has stimulated much research, found that married couples who shared highly connected, close-knit social networks had a higher degree of separateness in their married role patterns compared to spouses whose combined social networks were loose-knit and independent of each other, the latter having similar role patterns. Independent of the specific explanations that Laumann, Bott, and others have posited to explain these findings, these and other studies show the importance of network structures on the behavior of individuals. If, as Boissevain (1974) hopes, researchers can discover a relationship between the nature of the social and cultural environment and the structure of specific social networks, then network analysis represents a means for studying the influence of the environment on the behavior of individuals via the intervening factor of different network structures.

Social scientists traditionally have made sense of the social world by categorizing individuals according to various ascriptive and descriptive classificatory features (Craven and Wellman, 1973). Network researchers, in contrast, are concerned more with mapping out the complex (if not conceptually neat) reality of the interpersonal world surrounding individuals. As a result, network analyses have provided insight into the nature of the interpersonal world that has often contradicted established theories. More often than not, network studies have found that individuals' consequential social networks are larger and more diversified than commonly conceived. An example of such a study is Barnes' (1954) study of job seeking among the inhabitants of a Norwegian island parish, often considered the pioneer work in the study of social networks. The island society has two sides: a traditional, home-bound one and a more modern, sea-going one. Contrary to what Barnes expected from traditional sociological theories, boys born into one side of the society are likely to find work on either side. Barnes found that he could predict which type of work a boy would find and choose not on the basis of his family's work, but rather on the basis of the work done by members of his social network, which typically cut across these two sides of the society.

Another example of network analysis that challenges traditional concepts is that done by a group of anthropologists who study "kin-family networks." These writers claim that, increasingly, the tightly bounded nuclear family has been giving way in urban society to kin-family networks composed of nuclear families "bound together by affectional ties and choice" (Sussman and Burchinal, 1962). They believe that the kin family is better suited to the exigencies of contemporary life, and that major social developments, such as the shortened work week (leaving more leisure time), the development of high-speed highways, and the telephone (facilitating visiting and quick and frequent communication), help to explain the widespread emergence of kin family networks. Leichter and Mitchell's (1967) extensive study of ten New York City Jewish families confirmed some of the notions related to kin family networks. Leichter and Mitchell found extensive relationships among kin in these families; each family recognized an average of 241 kin. Women maintained much of the contact and did so over the telephone. They found that for each kinship event a different set of kin may be relevant, thus underscoring the element of choice in the functioning of kin family networks. Although some social scientists dispute the claim that kin family networks have replaced the nuclear family as the primary family structure in urban society (for example, Gibson, 1972), most do agree that kin family networks are particularly important in the lives of the increasing numbers of single, widowed, and divorced individuals in society.[5]

In addition to providing insight into the structure and composition of the personal communities of individuals, another potential advantage of network analysis is that it provides a means for studying the reality of substantial changes in people's social networks over time, the importance of which is reflected in Shulman's (1972) finding that, over a two-year period, 50 percent of the "intimates" of the Toronto residents he studied had changed. Network maps of the interpersonal alignments and structures existing at different points in time can be compiled, for instance, and

[5] Both the Essex and kin-family network are "mesh" networks, in the sense that all involved individuals experience a common identity and have "call" on each other. Individuals in them exchange resources and experience a sense of community. The outstanding difference is that the Essex network functions in the domain of the work world, which has a very different set of norms and goals than does the social sphere. It is helpful, however, to think of the Essex network as attempting to change the rules and common assumptions that guide thinking and action in the work world in order to facilitate the type of resource exchange that is more frequently experienced in the familial and social spheres.

then contrasted to analyze changes over time. A simplified version of one type of such study was carried out by Jongman (1973) in an African village. All interpersonal relationships in the African society he studied could clearly be identified as one of five culturally defined types. Jongman mapped out all household interrelationships that existed prior to and after a major dispute between two powerful leaders in the village, and was able to posit explanations for the realignments resulting from the dispute as a function of the initial network map. Jongman's study represents but one of many ways in which network mappings could be utilized to introduce the time element into the study of the interpersonal world.

Another extremely important potential advantage of network conceptualizations and analysis is that they are capable of providing a relatively complex, wholistic picture of the structure and functioning of the interpersonal environment. Different social science disciplines traditionally have singled out specific aspects of the interpersonal world for study. As often occurs when complex phenomena are broken up into discrete and specialized parts, the social scientist focusing on one aspect of the interpersonal environment and specific types of individuals and behaviors sometimes overemphasized that aspect of the interpersonal world at the expense of others, and often achieved a limited, inaccurate understanding of the relationship between that part and the whole, and of the inevitable interrelatedness and interdependency of that part with other diverse parts. The conceptualization and mapping out of total networks, in contrast, promise to force researchers to deal with the existence of the large number and diversity of parts in the whole, and to begin to realize how any one aspect or partial network is inevitably intertwined with and affected by other aspects and partial networks. The analysis of such far-reaching and diverse total networks holds out the possibility of a broadened and more integrated understanding of the interrelationships between diverse segments of the contemporary interpersonal world.

Organizational Interrelationships

An organization, broadly defined, is any collectivity of individuals with defined goals and identifiable criteria for membership.

A list of important types of organizations in a community would include business organizations, educational and human service institutions, governmental bodies and agencies, voluntary associations, labor unions, and political parties. In the recent past, most organizations functioned relatively autonomously, and had direct and indirect relationships and contacts with only a limited number of other organizations clearly related in function. Increasingly since World War II, however, interrelationships among organizations have expanded rapidly, and important relationships occur with diverse types of organizations spanning consumer, product, service, functional, and public-private sector boundaries and constituencies. Similarly, the influence on organizational functioning of interactions among organizations not directly connected to an organization has dramatically increased. As in the interpersonal realm, organizational interrelationships have become increasingly complex, far-reaching, diverse, and more likely to evolve rapidly over time.

The historical factors behind these developments are many, and closely related to developments in society at large. The expanding role of state and federal government in the functioning of local communities represents one specific factor, as does the substantial increase in the number of business, service, voluntary, and governmental organizations. One particularly crucial change in society in recent years, emphasized by Emery and Trist (1965), was that organizations were increasingly functioning within "turbulent" environments—rapidly changing, complexly interconnected environments that affect the functioning of single organizations but exist outside the realm of their control. One consequence observed by Emery and Trist was that large, single organizations were declining in numbers and, to better deal with the increasingly complex and unwieldy external environment, were forming "clusters" with other organizations.

Evan (1966) and Warren (1967) were the first social scientists to delineate specific concepts to describe a set of interacting organizations. Evan, noting the general neglect of the study of relations among organizations, offered the concept of *organization set* as a point of departure for such studies. The term is based on Merton's (1957) concept of *role set* (the complex of role relationships the occupant of a given status possesses). Evan states, "I shall take as the unit of analysis an organization, or a class of organizations, and trace its interactions with the network of organizations in its environment." Warren, drawing on Lewin's concept of "field" ("A totality of coexisting facts which are conceived of as mutually interdependent"), proposes the concept of "interorganizational field." He explains, "The concept of interorganizational field is based upon the observation that the interaction between two organizations is affected, in part at least, by the nature of the organizational pattern or network within which they find themselves."

Turk (1970) and Baker and Schulberg (1970) independently adopted the term *interorganizational network* to refer to the interrelationships among organizations. A number of authors have followed their lead in utilizing this term rather than *interorganizational field* and *organization set*. What is meant by the concept, however, remains basically unchanged from Evan's and Warren's characterizations, as evident in Benson's (1975) discussion of the concept: "The basic unit of analysis is the network of organizations. . . . The organizations in a network may be linked directly or indirectly. Some networks, for example, may consist of a series of organizations linked by multiple direct ties to each other. Others may be characterized by a clustering or centering of linkages around one or a few mediating or controlling organizations. Networks may thus be quite varied and their characteristics should be the object of explanation."

Interest in the study of organizational networks is a recent development, and there does not yet exist a clearly defined body of work, as does exist for social networks.[6] Empirical studies of organizational networks in particular are few in number. Nonetheless, it is our belief, and the belief of a number of interorganizational researchers, that network conceptualizations and analyses offer a

---

[6] Although this statement is true for the literature on networks, it should be remembered that many of our oldest laws, particularly those concerned with antitrust and conspiracies for price fixing, were based on findings of effective interorganizational networks within and among different sectors of business, finance, and industry. And if these laws are no less needed today than decades ago, it speaks to the fact that interorganizational networks were and are facts of life. If research on organizational networks has only recently come to the fore, it is another example of social scientists becoming aware of the obvious.

most useful and insightful means for viewing and understanding the complex world of organizational interrelationships. Just as is the case with social networks, organizational network concepts and analyses promise to be particularly helpful in studying the ways in which organizations differentially utilize direct, "weak," and indirect network ties to achieve goals; the ways in which such ties influence, limit, and constrain organizational functioning; the relationship between the structure of different organizational networks and organizational functioning; changes in organizational network composition and structure over time; and the diverse compositional and functional elements of total organizational networks, and the interrelationships among these elements. In the following discussion, we emphasize the potential contribution of network conceptualizations and analyses to an understanding of the organizational world, by singling out for brief discussion two important aspects of interorganizational functioning.

One crucial aspect of contemporary community functioning concerns the ability of diverse, interrelated organizations in a community effectively to coordinate activities and at the same time to achieve individual organizational and community goals. The study of the role of indirect and "weak" linkages, examination of the differential influence of different network structures and diversities of composition, and explicit analyses of changing network configurations over time all represent means of increasing an understanding of the dynamics and dilemmas of coordination among organizations. A network-related conceptualization of the effectiveness of interorganizational coordination is represented in the work of Aiken and Alford (1970). They hypothesize that the existence of complex interorganizational networks connecting community centers of power increase the capacity for coordination, innovation, and the attraction of federal funds, and that such networks are least likely to exist in expanding, rapidly changing communities lacking historically based, stable interorganizational linkages. The authors believe that the various centers of power within such historically based networks are most likely to have had the time to accumulate experience and information about the community system, and thus to be able to work out effective patterns of interaction. Network conceptualizations, mapping, and analyses will help refine and test such hypotheses, and give rise to others concerning diverse aspects of interorganizational coordination.

Another example of a promising area for network research is the study of the role that interpersonal contacts and relationships play in interorganizational functioning. Many writers have stressed the importance of informal, far-reaching networks of individuals in the functioning of interorganizational networks. Craven and Wellman (1973), for instance, state that formal organizational arrangements are too inflexible and cumbersome to carry out the complex, flexible coordination required in contemporary urban settings, and they claim that such formal arrangements are "always supplemented—and often supplanted—by informal interpersonal networks."[7] Evan (1974) emphasizes the need for the development of cross-cutting, far-reaching human networks of "boundary personnel" in multinational organizations and international professional associations to achieve coordination and integration of the economic and organizational international system. Schön (1971) notes that federal agencies are often tightly "bounded" and completely isolated from other federal agencies, that most interagency measures fail, and that informal networks of people are "often the chief means by which agencies can be coordinated in working on new problems that cut across their boundaries." The study of interpersonal networks in interorganizational relations is clearly important.

Curtis and Zurcher (1973) carried out one of the few studies that examined, albeit in a simplified fashion, both the organizational and interpersonal aspects of an organizational network. They compared the organizational and interpersonal networks of two antipornography organizations located in towns in different parts of the country. Although the primary zone of both networks

---

[7] This was a very significant point in the rationale of the Essex network. The Essex network was explicitly one consisting of individuals rather than agencies. Almost all network members were affiliated with formal organizations, but they did not "officially" represent them. It was our hope that to the extent that these members were influenced by their network activities they might over time be a force for change within their agencies. Our experience with the Essex network confirms Craven and Wellman's conclusion that formal organizational arrangements are an obstacle to coordination and mutually beneficial resource exchange.

was composed of similar numbers and types of organizations, the authors found that the more effective organization had, among a number of differentiating factors, a greater quantity of individual members involved in other organizations in the network, a greater quantity of members holding administrative positions in these organizations, and a greater homogeneity of membership. There were a number of other factors that clearly had major impact on the functioning of the two organizations (for example, more specified and realistic goals) and the authors thus do not attempt to make causal statements related to their differential effectiveness. Future research, however, will hopefully be able to explore more intensively the role of different types and structures of formal and informal interpersonal networks in organizational network functioning.

To date, there has been little mapping and analysis of organizational networks. Organizational researchers appear completely unaware of the conceptual and analytical work that has been done on social networks, and they might benefit in important ways by reviewing this work. The impact of organizations and organizational networks on society is great, and the conceptualization and analysis of far-reaching, diversely composed, total interorganizational networks represent an important endeavor for the social science disciplines.

Intraorganizational Structure

The viable functioning of interorganizational networks, and of society, depends in part on the viable functioning of individual organizations. The functioning of organizations, in turn, depends in part on the adaptiveness and effectiveness of their internal structure of control, authority, and communication. Whereas the relatively autonomous organization of years back adapted well to a relatively static, hierarchical internal structure, the increasingly complex and rapidly changing external environment that increasingly confronts organizations (Emery and Trist, 1965) has made demands on organizations for more flexible and less hierarchical intraorganizational structures. Burns and Stalker (1961), for instance, in their book, *The Management of Innovation,* state that the unstable, rapidly changing conditions of the environment "give rise constantly to fresh problems and unforeseen requirements for action which cannot be broken down or distributed automatically [according to] . . . the functional roles defined within a hierarchical structure" (p. 121). They stress that, if a firm is to adapt, individuals must perform tasks in light of their knowledge of the firm as a whole, and jobs would lose much of their formal definitions in terms of methods, duties, and powers.[8] The result would be an internal configuration characterized by a lateral rather than a vertical direction of intraorganizational communication, and a communication that resembles consultation rather than command.

Burns and Stalker termed the flexible internal structure they described a "network structure of control, authority and communication." Many researchers have discussed the need for and emergence of such flexible, nonhierarchical, internal structures, and some have continued to use various network conceptualizations to describe them. Schön (1971) in his book, *Beyond the Stable State*, for instance, develops a broad-based concept of network as "a set of elements related to one another through multiple interconnections" and devotes a chapter to describing the emergence of intraorganizational networks within complex organizations he terms "business system firms." A "business system" is the complex network of diverse types of firms related to one another in the performance of a major social function, such as "keeping us in clean clothes." Whereas the traditional business firm evolved by combining companies manufacturing similar end products or those that link raw materials to a final consumer product, a business system firm emerges by organizing the entire network of organizations involved

---

[8] This point is similar to our belief that the Essex network had to remain as informal as possible in order to take advantage of opportunities as they presented themselves. The reader will recall that one of the characteristics of the Essex network we stressed was the unpredictability of the directions it could or would go. To the extent that the network took on the trappings of a formal organization, especially as a way to secure funding, to that extent, we felt, we would be constricting its capacity to act quickly and flexibly. If we take too "pure" a view of this problem, it reflects our past experience in trying to get formal organizations to make decisions, let alone take action. This may help the reader understand better why we have emphasized that ours was a network of individuals and not agencies.

into a business system. In order to achieve this, the business system firm has to develop an extremely flexible, responsive mode of functioning capable of adapting to and controlling continuous developments in the complex, rapidly changing, external network of firms. Such organizational functioning, according to Schön, depends on the design, development, and management of internal networks. Two important characteristics of these networks are that authority is dispersed throughout the network and information is available simultaneously at the important nodes of decision.

Hage (1974), in his study of the emergence of network structures within health and welfare settings, operationally distinguishes network from hierarchical structures, basing the distinction on the amount of self-initiated conferring that employees had with superiors in their department, superiors in other departments, and employees of lower or similar rank in other departments. He delineated four models of internal structures for organizations containing at least two departments and four levels of employees (that is, workers, supervisors, department heads, and executives). In the "single mechanical hierarchy," employees confer primarily with superiors directly above them. Employees in the "multiple mechanical hierarchy" have access to superiors located virtually anywhere in the organization, including other departments. In the "single organic network," there exists, in addition, a greater emphasis on downward conferring flows, and an emergence of a "criss-cross" pattern at several employee levels, in which workers at one level confer (up or down) with those at other levels in other departments. The "multiple organic network" is characterized by "criss-cross" conferring flows among all levels, and, in addition, horizontal linkages emerge, connecting workers of similar status in different departments. Basing his conclusions on correlational analyses of data obtained in interviews with employees at sixteen health and welfare settings, and an in-depth study of an evolving network structure in a general hospital, Hage suggests that organic network structures are most likely to evolve as an organization's structure becomes more diversified, as role specialization increases, and as power becomes more dispersed.

Hage's conception stresses that there is a continuum of possible internal structures of organizations, ranging from predominantly hierarchical to predominantly network, with varying degrees of network and hierarchical features in between. Kingdon (1973) describes an organizational form that simultaneously includes mechanical, hierarchical, and organic network forms. The matric organizational model consists of (1) a normal hierarchical system used for "functional" organizational needs, such as setting goals and allocating resources, and (2) nonhierarchical "project groups" composed of employees of diverse roles, used to carry out the actual technological tasks of the organization. The project groups are needed, since neither the management nor any single individual or group of individuals in the organization can deal with the rapidly evolving diversity of organizational needs and tasks. They function via an organic network structure of authority, control, and communication.

Intraorganizational structures seem to and may increasingly be changing, at least in some organizations, from ones in which power and authority are centralized and employee interactions relatively limited to one in which power and authority are more dispersed and individuals have significant reciprocal work interactions with diverse individuals spanning functional, departmental, and authority-related roles. These interrelationships are likely to change over time as conditions and organizational needs change. The intraorganizational world has changed in ways similar to the interpersonal and interorganizational, in that individuals and organizations in contemporary society have significant reciprocal relationships with diverse other actors, who span narrowly bounded, functionally specific role, group, and system categorizations. There are, of course, substantial differences between interorganizational or social network structures and intraorganizational ones—the membership of an intraorganizational network is very limited, since it can include only those who fall within the organizational boundary, and the network members all function in the context of shared superordinate goals and power of the organization. Although these important differences exist, it is our opinion that network conceptualizations, mappings, and analyses can fruitfully be applied to the study of intraorganizational structures, with many of the same advantages in vision and understanding described in the preceding section on social networks.

It is appropriate here to note that in the emerging literature on interorganizational and intraorganizational networks, there is scant attention (perhaps not surprising) to the personal values and needs of those in a network. The assumption seems to be either that these individual needs and values are congruent with those of the organization or that if they are not congruent, they must become secondary to or submerged by organizational values in the service of efficiency and productivity. Ironically, it is precisely the inefficiency of so many of these organizations, and the pervasive interpersonal conflicts within them, that have stimulated organizational restructuring and new network concepts, and yet the question of the role of values in these concepts has hardly been confronted. This we have tried to confront in the rationale and development of the Essex network, not from any stance of moral superiority, but from the assumption that to divorce personal values and needs from one's experience of work is to ensure personal frustration and the sense of unproductiveness. Without explicit confrontation of these issues, the increasing attention concepts of networks are getting may well become another unfortunate example of mindless immersion in technology and method. This is not to contradict the statement that network concepts can be fruitfully applied, but to enter a caveat based on what has so frequently happened with potentially new concepts and findings. This, of course, was the kind of lesson atomic scientists learned after Hiroshima and Nagasaki. If you do not begin with values, you end up regretting it.

Community Decision Making and Power Structures

As the world of interpersonal, interorganizational and intraorganizational relationships has become increasingly complex, so has the world of public sector decision making. Contemporary community and political leadership depends increasingly on the skill of creating and utilizing diverse networks of people, organizations, and resources. The more strategically located and far-reaching the networks manipulated by a leader, the more power and influence he wields. Whereas the successful public sector leader intuitively knows a great deal about the existence and functioning of diverse types of networks, social scientists who study public sector decision making processes have rarely made explicit use of network conceptions and analyses.

Social scientists traditionally have attempted to study community leadership by identifying individuals who were reported or observed to have control over important community decisions. Two major theories of community power structures dominate the literature. The "elitist" tradition maintains that a small group of individuals have essential control over the public decision-making process on all major issues. In contrast, the "pluralist" school believes that power is distributed among a number of organized community groups whose impact on and control over decision making in the community shifts, depending on the nature of the issue at hand. Walton (1966) analyzed thirty-three studies of community power and found a distinct relationship between research methodology and results. Elitist power structures tended to be discovered in research that used the "reputational" method, in which identification of community leaders was based on their reputed influence among community members who were interviewed. Pluralistic structures were most often found when an "issue-oriented" approach was used, which utilized historical, observational, and interviewing techniques to identify leaders who were involved in a number of different major community decisions.

An example of a network-related conceptualization of community power, and an alternate methodology to those used by the elitist and pluralistic schools, is present in the work of Perrucci and Pilisuk (1970). These authors believe that it is impossible for single individuals to command all the resources (for example, money, media, jobs) needed to influence or intimidate others into supporting them. Rather, they contend that the resources are dispersed among various community organizations and that the "power" needed to shape community decisions resides in the "interorganizational connections that may be mobilized in specific situations." The authors fault the researchers in the elitist and pluralistic traditions for focusing their attention on the discovery of particular individuals reputed or found to be involved in community decisions, rather than focusing on the discovery of "resource networks" and those individuals who have control over them.[9] Perrucci and Pilisuk

[9] Mrs. Dewar's role in the Essex network illustrates these contrasting approaches. From one standpoint, it could be said that her influence and power stemmed from her affluence and place in an elitist "establishment." From another standpoint, and one we think has some validity, it was her

suggest that one means of studying resource networks is to discover the organizational leaders in a community who hold executive positions in a number of organizations, since such overlapping executives represent one type of link between organizations and presumably can mobilize resources located in them. The authors present evidence that the executives in a midwestern community who held high positions in four or more organizations, when compared with those who held high positions in from one to three, had much more extensive social and business ties, were much more likely to be reputed or observed to have power, and linked together a tightly bounded network of organizations. While the authors do not present evidence that these individuals had control over the community's most important resource networks, their emphasis on viewing power, decision making, and leadership as dependent on control over and mobilization of extensive networks of people, organizations, and resources represents a promising beginning to utilizing network conceptualizations to understand and study community power structures.

A different and more methodologically sophisticated manner in which network analysis can be used to examine community power structures is represented in the work of Laumann and Pappi (1973). They identified the "community influentials" in a middle-sized city by interviewing "well-informed" community members. They then asked each of the influentials to choose from the compiled list of influentials three individuals with whom they had the most frequent and most intimate (1) social, (2) business/professional, and (3) community-affairs-oriented relations. Then, utilizing recent advances in the mathematical techniques of directed graph theory and smallest-space analysis, they were able to graphically represent these interrelationships in the forms of three circular network graphs. Each influential is located at a specific point on the graph, and lies closest to the individuals with whom he stated he had the most intimate and frequent relationships. The graph is divided into sectors representing different foci of community activity, and the most influential individuals are located most centrally in their

---

knowledge of and role in "resource networks" that enabled her to develop and nurture the quick growth of the Essex network. As we pointed out earlier, the elitist view would tend to gloss over the difficulties she had by virtue of her lack of professional credentials.

spheres of influence, since central locations have more direct access through the least number of "steps" to all other individuals in the sector. (Each "step" represents a direct linkage between individuals chosen as one of the three influentials with whom an intimate relationship existed.) Individuals and groups of individuals representing opposing interests and having few direct or indirect linking ties tended to be located far apart on the graph. The authors were able to draw lines dividing the community affairs graph network into the different opposing coalitions that interviewees had identified as existing on five important community issues. The study demonstrates, in a limited way, the potential usefulness of network graphs for depicting power structures, coalitions, and cleavages. Laumann and Pappi note that more extensive analysis of the data in the graphs could be done, to study the internal structures of the various coalitions, their influence resources, and their preferred leadership strategies. In addition, they state that graph networks represent meaningful "snapshots" of a community's consensus and cleavage structure at a particular point in time, and, if periodically compiled and juxtaposed, they could be used to describe and study stability and change in the community's influence structure over time.

Whereas Perrucci and Pilisuk and Laumann and Pappi studied the network linkages that exist within communities, another potentially important focus for network conceptualization and analysis is the impact of extracommunity institutions and forces on community leaders, functioning, and decision making. Merton (1957) delineated two types of influential leaders in communities, local and "cosmopolitan" influentials. The latter tend not to have extensive networks in the local community, but instead are oriented to affairs outside the community. A number of researchers in France have studied the extracommunity networks of local officials (Clark, 1973). They found that many local officials spend considerable amounts of time developing networks of contacts with national agency officials who are responsible for decisions affecting their local communities. The nature of these networks vary, depending in part on the "resources" available to the local official. For instance, a Communist mayor may develop an extracommunity network via the party structure, whereas a bridge inspector might first develop contacts in his area of expertise, and then try to expand it to other ministries. Turk (1970) found, in his comparative study of antipoverty networks in the nation's 130 largest cities, that the more extensive the "extralocal" organizational linkages a city has, the more War on Poverty funds the city received. (Turk operationalized "extralocal" organizational linkages as the number of national headquarters of federal agencies located in the city.) Clark (1973), in his review of literature on community decision making, states that more detailed studies of the different types of extracommunity networks and of their impact on community functioning are needed.

In addition to community leadership and extracommunity forces, a network conceptualization of community power needs to take into account the impact of average citizens and grass roots organization on community decision making. Researchers traditionally have tended to account for the ability of neighborhoods and communities to organize successfully on the basis of personal, subcultural, historical, and political factors. Granovetter (1973) claims that a more detailed and incisive analysis would take into account the quantity and quality of network "bridging" ties in the community under study. A "bridging" tie, according to Granovetter, is a "weak" (that is, nonintense, acquaintance-level) tie that effectively "bridges" the gap between cohesive, tightly knit, social groups and cliques. He speculates that the reason the West End Boston residents in Gans' (1962) *Urban Villagers* were unable to form a community organization to fight urban renewal was that there were no bridging ties between the isolated cliques of the neighborhood, and thus it lacked the cohesiveness necessary for concerted action. Granovetter contrasts the unsuccessful actions of the West End residents with those in the Charlestown section of Boston, who successfully organized against the urban renewal plan. He notes that, unlike the West Enders, those in Charlestown had a rich organizational life, with many residents working within the area, thus substantially increasing the probability of the development of bridging ties. Although there is no empirical data in the community studies literature on the role of weak, bridging ties in community organization, Granovetter predicts that such research would show that the more local "bridges" in a community and the greater their strength, the greater the likelihood that a community will be able to achieve the cohesiveness needed for successful organization.

The studies noted here only begin to suggest some ways in which a network conceptualization of community decision making can provide meaningful insights and a broader understanding of this complex area. The important point to note is that interpersonal, organizational, and intraorganizational networks within and outside of communities have become, and will increasingly become, complexly interwoven, and that one potential means for coming to a better understanding of the implications of these developments on community decision making is through network conceptualization, mapping, and analysis.

Recapitulation

We have been emphasizing two general points. The first was to underscore the obvious: All aspects of the contemporary world, ranging from the physical/technological, to the social/interpersonal, the intra- and interorganizational, and the world of public sector decision making, have changed dramatically in the direction of increasing complexity, fluidity, and interrelatedness of the units involved. More so than ever before, significant interactions in society are continually taking place among diverse units spanning role, functional, and geographic boundaries. The functioning of any one organization or individual is increasingly dependent on interactions among units with which the affected individual or organization has no direct contact.

The second point was that social scientists in diverse fields have independently adopted the concept of network to make sense of the complex contemporary interrelatedness of society. It is their belief that network conceptualizations and analytical techniques have a distinctive potential for contributing to our understanding of the functioning of the contemporary world. Although there are some differences in the network concept developed in different fields, in the first part of this section we derived a generalized concept of network that cut across these fields, and briefly contrasted the primary characteristics of this concept with the more traditional and "bounded" concepts of group and system.

The generalized concept of network we derived conceives a network as a structural entity that centers around a specified focal unit (for example, individual, family, organization) and includes all those units with which the focal unit has direct and indirect interrelationships. In direct contrast with tightly bounded group and system conceptualizations, the only characteristic that all members of a network have in common is their relationship (direct or indirect) with the focal unit; there is no clear external boundary surrounding a network, and the individuals, families, or organizations within a focal unit's network do not necessarily have interrelationships with each other. A primary distinguishing characteristic of network interactions is that they are relatively "all-encompassing" and "far-reaching"—an interaction affecting any one unit will tend to spread and have ramifications that ultimately affect many network units. A primary distinguishing characteristic of network composition is that a very large number of units extremely diverse in role, function, and type are involved in a focal unit's network— the number and diversity of the network units that significantly affect, and are potentially available for utilization by the focal unit, challenge both everyday and social science conceptions.

The term *network analysis* refers to the diverse array of techniques used by different researchers to depict and analyze the interrelationships and interactions among the units involved in a network. One major analytical task common to many network researchers has been to analyze the structural characteristics of the network. One important structural dimension that has been found to have an important impact on network functioning is the "density" of the network—the extent to which individuals or organizations who have direct relationships with the focal unit interact and are known to each other. Specific network analytical techniques used to depict and study the differential interrelationships among units range from simple matrix analyses to extremely complex, computerized "mapping" of large networks. The methodology used to collect data on networks, and to characterize the nature, types, degrees of intensity, and importance of relationships within networks vary from discipline to discipline and study to study.

Network conceptualizations and analyses offer distinctive advantages for those interested in understanding contemporary societal interactions and interrelatedness. The lack of theoretical presuppositions in network conceptions and the emphasis on mapping out total networks maximizes the probability that the researcher will discover and be forced to deal with the complex, if not conceptually neat, reality of interrelationships in the real world. Network conceptualizations, mappings, and analyses centered on focal units encourage and provide a concrete means for the study of the ways in which individual people and organizations differentially affect and manipulate their network environments. In turn, the analysis of network structures and the study of the relationship between external environment and network structure, and of network structure and individual or organizational functioning, provide a concrete means for the analysis of the influence of the environment, via network structure, on the individual. The study of the use of weak, bridging ties and of indirect linkages on individual or organizational functioning, will provide insight into a most important and relatively unexplored aspect of societal functioning. Network analysis also provides a concrete means, through the delineation and analysis of network configurations in an area over time, for researchers to study change in individual and organizational interactions over time. Finally, the mapping and study of the total networks of individuals and organizations provide a potential means for developing a wholistic view of the interrelationships of diverse segments of the interpersonal or interorganizational environment that traditionally are studied in isolation.

In our attempt to discern a generalized concept of network across fields, we chose to focus on specific structural and compositional aspects of networks. We deliberately did not attempt to define a generalized concept in terms of the nature and process of interactions among network units. There were some general aspects of network processes that seemed to apply across fields, such as a "far-reachingness" of impact of network events and a "fluidity" as networks constantly evolve and change over time. However, network conceptualizations and research have only recently begun in the social sciences, and, to date, there is little theoretical or empirical work across fields that substantiates these or other specific facts about the why, when, where, and how of direct and indirect interactions among large numbers of diverse individuals and organiza tions in our complexly interrelated society.

A Historical Note

Assuming that network structures have been evolving in society for some time, why is it only in recent years that social scientists have begun to focus explicitly on this phenomenon in a substantial way? (There have been individuals, of course, who prior to the emergence of network concepts perceived the importance of the widespread interrelationships of modern society, and even some social scientists who adopted the term *network* and discussed some of its specific attributes [for example, Moreno, 1934]. Such work, however, was not widespread.) One general background factor helping to explain the recentness of this development is that, especially since World War II, the technological, social, and demographic developments of the last century have surfaced in ways that have forced individuals, social scientists included, to realize that indeed it is a small world in which developments on one side of the globe, or nation, or city, affect those on the other side. As this general awareness of the complex interrelatedness in the world became implanted in the minds of social scientists, they have come to be increasingly predisposed to perceive the interrelated nature of particular phenomena they are studying. (The emergence of general systems theories, emphasizing the interrelatedness of phenomena within all the sciences—physical, biological, social— may also have helped to stimulate this development.)

A second, more specific, factor helping to explain the recentness of this development is the post-World War II emergence of technology capable of analyzing the complex interrelationships among the large number of units that make up networks. The computer, for instance, has played an important role in applied technical fields such as operations research and city planning, since it allows researchers to take into account extensive amounts of information affecting networks and network flows. Similarly, developments in mathematics such as smallest-space analysis and directed graph theory have begun to allow social scientists to depict graphically and analyze the interrelationships among a large number of interacting individuals or organizations (Levine, 1972). Such advances have led to an increased understanding about and use of network concepts, and have begun to make possible the use of complex networks as dependent and independent variables in research studies. In addition, as technology has helped applied fields to surmount complex technical problems, it has simultaneously contributed to the development of increasingly complex, interrelated networks in society.

A third and perhaps more directly influential factor is the change in the modes of research, and the role of researchers, in various fields. During World War II, scientists were called on to solve essential technical military problems that forced them to deal with the movement of goods and personnel—a task for which the conceptualization of networks was essential. Following the war, these and other scientists were asked by industry to solve essential peacetime problems of efficient organizational operations—again, networks were central to this work. Moreover, while scientists were forced to conceptualize networks in order to meet these societal needs, the surmounting of these problems made possible the development of ever more complex networks. The change in role from "pure" to applied scientist stimulated the development and conceptualization of various types of networks.

One important change in the mode of research of a number of social scientists from the 1940s onwards has been the emphasis on descriptive field studies rather than survey, macrotheoretical work. Another important change was the post-World War II development of intraorganizational and, later, interorganizational studies as important social science research and applied disciplines. A third important change has been the focus of some social scientists in the last fifteen years on research centered on understanding and evaluating social and human service change efforts, and the adoption of change agent roles by some of these individuals. It is not coincidental that the social scientists who have developed and most often utilized network concepts have, for the most part, been descriptive fields researchers or those involved in applied individual, organizational, or social change efforts. It is such individuals who are forced to deal with the everyday world as it exists. They are also most likely to realize that when change efforts are unsuccessful, as were many in recent years, it is often due to the reality that individuals or settings that were the focus of change function within and are deeply affected by complex, interrelated, rapidly changing networks. The interplay of theory and practice that occurs when social scientists "take to the field" stimulates the development of realistic conceptions and knowledge about the nature of society.

11

Network Conceptualizations and Change

〜〜〜〜〜〜〜〜〜〜〜〜〜〜〜〜〜〜

In this chapter we review several areas of social science research that utilize various network conceptualizations to understand important aspects of individual and social change. First is a review of literature in two social science subfields concerned with studying naturally occurring processes within society directly related to social and individual change—the diffusion of innovation, and the social support provided to troubled individuals. Then there is a look at some literature in which network conceptualizations are used to describe or propose actual strategies for change—strategies for intervention within social networks, and for intervention within the human service, business, and governmental sectors of society. The reviews are intended to present information and ideas hopefully of substantive interest to the reader,

157

and to demonstrate the potential usefulness and importance of network conceptualizations in various areas related to social change.

The Diffusion of Innovation

The effective diffusion of new ideas and practices represents a crucial problem in contemporary society, one that strikes at the very heart of individual and community functioning and change. The study of the diffusion of innovations constitutes a major social science research area, encompassing seven major research traditions—anthropology, sociology, rural sociology, education, medical sociology, communications, and marketing (Rogers and Shoemaker, 1971). It is a rapidly expanding area of study, as reflected in the fact that between 1964 and 1972 the number of published research works in the field tripled, reaching a total of 1,500 at the time of Rogers' and Shoemaker's review of the diffusion of innovation literature. After a time in which numerous change efforts were initiated and few succeeded, the importance of the study of the process by which innovations spread, and of the factors that affect their passage and implementation, has become increasingly apparent to both researchers and social change agents.

Rogers and Shoemaker define a communication network as "any number of individuals in a system, starting with a source person and sequentially continuing through all the related individuals who are his direct or indirect receivers" (1971, p. 82). It would appear natural that the concept of network, and the detailed study of communication networks, would occupy an important place in the diffusion literature. In fact, however, the concept does not appear in the literature until the publication of Katz and Lazarsfeld's *Personal Influence,* in 1955, more than half a century after sociologists first became interested in the problem of how information flowed through society. The utilization of network relationships as the empirical unit of analysis first occurs around the same time, with the publication of Coleman, Katz, and Menzel's (1957) "The Diffusion of an Innovation Among Physicians." Prior to this, researchers had used individuals as the unit of analysis, utilizing survey-oriented research that tended to focus on individual, intrapersonal variables rather than on network, social-structural ones. The work of Coleman, Katz, and Menzel (see also 1966), although an advance over previous research, is only a limited one, since they operationalized the concept network to refer only to simple dyadic pairs of individuals. The authors recognized the limited nature of their work, and stated, "To analyze pairs of individuals instead of single individuals may seem like a very modest step in the direction of the analysis of networks of social relations. And so it is; it would be more satisfactory, and truer to the complexity of actual events, if it were possible to use larger chains and more ramified systems of social relations as the unit of analysis. But so little developed are the methods for the analysis of social process, that it seems best to be content with pairs of relationships" (pp. 113–114). Unfortunately, methodological problems and the absence of sophisticated techniques for the analysis of large networks have continued to restrict the study of networks in the field primarily to the study of dyadic relationships (Rogers and Shoemaker, 1971).

The diffusion research literature does, nonetheless, document the importance of networks in the diffusion process. Perhaps most important, it indicates that different types of network channels, linkages, and diffusion roles differentially affect the effectiveness and nature of the diffusion process. Some examples of research related to these points are presented in the following paragraphs.

A communication channel is the "means by which the message gets from the source to the receiver" (Rogers and Shoemaker, 1971, p. 24). The one-step model of mass communications flow emphasizes that new ideas and practices are communicated directly, albeit with different degrees of effectiveness, to individuals through the channels of mass media networks. The two-step flow model, in contrast, states that the mass media channels are often responsible for communicating innovations to influential "opinion leaders," but that interpersonal network channels between these individuals and their less active associates are responsible for the passage of the innovations to the larger public. Eighteen research studies confirm the finding that mass media network channels are relatively more important in providing knowledge about an innovation, and interpersonal network channels more important in persuading individuals to adopt it (Rogers and Shoemaker, 1971).

An important question for community functioning concerns

the channels through which important organizational and public leaders receive change-related ideas. Saunders and Reppucci (in press) studied the "learning networks" of three types of human service organizational leaders—superintendents of juvenile correctional facilities, principals of elementary schools and directors of institutions for the mentally retarded—and found that these administrators utilized different network channels. Interview data revealed that the superintendents relied most heavily on "extrasystemic" channels, such as conferences, outside consultants, and graduate school courses, for the acquisition of new ideas; the principals relied mostly on reading professional journals and books; and the directors were most likely to depend on "systemic" channels, such as staff resources and institutional meetings. Only 8 percent of the superintendents and 17 percent of the directors indicated that reading was a major channel for receiving new ideas.

Granovetter (1973) claims that "strong" and "weak" network linkages play different roles in the diffusion process. A "weak tie," in contrast to a "strong" one, is characterized by a lesser investment of time, emotional intensity, intimacy (mutual confiding), and exchange of services in the relationship. Granovetter hypothesizes that "the weaker one's ties to some individual X, the fewer *other* people with whom one has ties will also have ties to X! . . . People tied weakly to each other move in different circles." A loosely knit network, then, is one where most of one's friends do not know each other, whereas in a tightly knit network most of one's friends are also friends of one another. Granovetter speculates that information passed into a closely knit network will spread rapidly to those people within the network, but probably not very quickly beyond the network. In contrast, a message transmitted within a loosely knit network will probably reach larger numbers of people outside the network, since the weak ties will effectively transmit the message outside the social circles of the network. The message, however, will probably take a longer time to reach any particular person within the loosely knit network.

As indirect evidence in support of these assertions, Granovetter reviews the results of several of Milgram's "small-world" studies (Milgram, 1967). In one of these studies, arbitrarily chosen white individuals were told to send a booklet to a specified, unknown, black target person via someone the sender knows personally who is more likely than himself to know the target individual (Korte and Milgram, 1970). Each recipient of the booklet then becomes the sender to a next individual, until the chain is completed. Granovetter notes that in 50 percent of the successfully completed chains, in contrast to 26 percent of the incomplete ones, the white person "crossed" the racial barrier via weak network ties (that is, via acquaintances rather than friends), indicating that the weaker ties afford more "reach." He comments that in cases where the first black recipient was a friend, it is less likely that he would be well connected in black circles, whereas if he were only an acquaintance his primary links were more likely to be among other blacks, facilitating the ultimate contact of the target black person. Granovetter also speculates that the "early adopters" of risky or controversial innovations will most likely be marginal persons with many weak ties—marginal because central figures will want to protect their reputations (Becker, 1970), and with weak ties because an initially unpopular innovation will only spread to a few cliques via strong ties and then stop there. Only weak ties will ensure the early widespread exposure and adoption needed for a risky or deviant innovation to effectively "catch on" and spread in a chain reaction. Unfortunately, the diffusion research literature focuses almost entirely on strong ties, and there is little direct evidence to test this or related hypotheses about the differential roles of strong and weak network linkages in the diffusion process.

Schön (1971) criticizes the traditional "central-periphery" model of the diffusion of innovation and describes an alternative model based on the functioning of "self-transforming networks." The central-periphery model, according to Schön, holds that an innovation is basically complete in its essentials prior to diffusion, and is moved out from a center, through radial spokes, to a periphery, through a carefully managed process. The network in this model usually consists of dyadic links connecting one individual to the next, and its "role" is to "pass on" the innovation from node to node (that is, individual to individual).

Schön believes that innovations, such as discrete products, that produce only minimal disruptions in existing systems follow this classic central-periphery process of diffusion. He claims, however, that innovations that precipitate systemic changes diffuse through a much more complex process and involve cross-cutting, far-reaching networks, which play an active role in the development of the innovation. Two examples of such systemic innovations that Schön details are the spread of the granite industry in New England in the nineteenth and twentieth centuries and the interrelated social movements of the 1960s concerned with causes such as civil rights, black power, peace, the Vietnam War, student rights, and disarmament. The "Movement" involved numerous groups operating at both local and national levels. Conceptualizing the Movement as a system for diffusing new ideas and practices, Schön notes that, unlike in the central-periphery model, there was no stable, centrally established theory, technology, or methodology diffusing from a single, clearly established center to a periphery. Rather, he describes the Movement as a "loosely connected, shifting and evolving whole in which centers come and go and messages emerge, rise and fall." Schön attributes its ability to retain national connectedness and cohesiveness in the face of changes in leadership and messages over time to its "infrastructure technology," which included elements such as television, jet transport, an underground press, telephones, records, tapes, radio, and extensive informal networks of students, blacks, and radicals. Thus new ideas and practices were continually received, evolved, and dispersed via interrelated media and interpersonal network channels. Schön observes that the Movement and the business system firm, although apparently antithetical, both represent self-transforming network models that increasingly characterize the nature and process of the diffusion of innovation in contemporary society.

Social Support

Researchers from social and community psychiatry, sociology, and social psychology have focused study on networks in relation to the natural helping relationship. Some have used the concept of network to illuminate aspects of support from the natural environment for a person in actual crisis. Boswell (1969), for instance, utilized the concept to understand the coping process for urban Central African families who were mourning a dead family member.

Boswell centers his discussion on widows and argues that *network* is far more accurate than *kin* as a term to encompass the people who help them. Boswell makes explicit the importance of the situational context in assessing the importance of any one individual to a widow. Network analysis allowed him to include central hostile relationships in his picture, and he argues that these connections are crucial for understanding the widow's behavior in the crisis. Speck, Barr, Eisenman, Foulks, Goldman, and Lincoln (1972) were interested in social support for young "dropouts" in urban American settings. They found that peers, rather than families, provided the needed social support; indeed, that the networks of these youth were heavily weighted with peers. The youth themselves did not see kin as providing social support. Levine (1972) focused on the kin network that was available to hospitalized cardiac patients. Lee (1969) studied acquaintance networks and information networks instrumental in the search for an illegal abortionist. Lee emphasized that a woman's network will have had certain experiences with respect to abortion and will lack others, and this selective information in her network will influence how the woman seeking the abortion perceives her situation.

Some investigators have utilized the concept of network to understand nonprofessional influences on the decision to seek professional or paraprofessional help, and then on the ability to obtain the help. McKinlay (1973) studied the network of friends and relatives who help a person decide to seek professional help. Collins, Emlen, and Watson (1969) studied the network of people who help a person find paraprofessional day-care services.

Researchers have investigated natural helping relationships without network analysis. A comparison of the other approaches with the network approach demonstrates the usefulness of network analysis in this area. In studies that do not look at networks, the investigators generally limit their work to relationships between two or three people in a contrived field setting or a laboratory setting (for example, Merrens, 1973). The network studies, on the other hand, clearly show that helping as it occurs in the "real world" typically involves many individuals from diverse settings. In some studies, investigators report about helping with reference only to kin. Boswell (1969) argues against focusing on kin to understand helping in modern urban settings. He states that "in rural and small communities it has been possible to isolate the various duties and obligations vested in certain individuals who stand in a particular political, kinship or economic relationship to those involved. The potential fluidity of urban society largely prevents such an analysis in town, because the availability of kin and 'big men' to every family may be completely different and no common pattern of duties emerge for various categories of kin and others" (p. 255). Shapiro (1969) studied helping relationships in single-room occupancies (SRO's) in New York City and found several natural "leaders" who provided a great amount of gratification, control of disruptive behavior, and support functions for many occupants of the SRO's. However, while this analysis looks at natural helping, it does not look at the whole network of helping relationships for an individual, but again focuses on dyadic relationships between helper and helpee. Thus, elements of the actual experience of the helpee are missing without a more complete network analysis. Another example of the need for the network concept can be seen in two studies of the decision whether or not to seek professional help. Liberman (1965) sampled fifty-two individuals to discover factors leading to psychiatric hospitalization. He does not utilize networks, but looks at the influence of a single third party in making the decision of hospitalization. He lists the resources that were directly responsible for this decision: medical doctor, 18; police, 17; psychiatrist or clinic, 6; mental hospital, 4; and social agency, general hospital, or lawyer, 7. On the other hand, McKinlay (1973) used networks to understand why an individual seeks even the professional help that pressures towards psychiatric hospitalization. Hammer (1964) used the person's social network in understanding the potential for helping a person seen as deviant. She suggests that the "actual or anticipated responses that their [the helpers'] behavior concerning the patient may elicit from the other people they interact with, who in turn are affected by their own networks of interaction" will provide pressure against helping the individual personally and for psychiatric hospitalization. Thus, by using networks, the issue of hospitalization is perceived more broadly. In fact, Caplan (1974) and Tolsdorf (1975), in trying to understand why some individuals cope successfully in a crisis situation while others do not, used the availability of networks and people's willingness to use them as major explanatory factors.

Social Network Intervention Strategies

Human service professionals have written about strategies for intervention into social networks on behalf of individuals. If networks are indeed a basic social structure in our society, then an attempt to intervene in the interpersonal environment of an individual might best be done with as much of the network as possible. Six such intervention strategies were found in the literature, and we have ranked them in terms of increasing breadth of community involvement by the professional. First, family therapists have expanded their work into the social network of schizophrenics. Second, social scientists have worked with large peer groups of urban "dropouts" in an attempt to reach these youth effectively. Third, an institutional psychotherapist has tried to change a resident's network that he conceptualizes as a support for deviant or prosocial behavior. Fourth, community mental health practitioners have moved beyond the environments of families and schools to include all the essential people in a client's network to work towards a solution of the problems. Fifth, mental health people have intervened in networks of people in a crisis situation. Sixth, community mental health professionals have intervened in naturally occurring day-care networks to improve their scope and functioning. In each of these cases, people were the focus of the change agent's efforts. Clearly, further applications of network ideas are possible towards the goal of individual change. Generally, all of these change strategies take seriously the idea that important interpersonal relationships reflect a network structure in our society.

First, Speck and his colleagues (Speck, 1967; Attneave and Speck, 1974; Speck and Rueveni, 1969) make use of the social networks of adolescent schizophrenics in an intense short-term treatment strategy. The therapeutic team assembles the schizophrenic individual, his family, all other available kin, and friends and neighbors of the individual together in the person's living room.

The network is typically restricted to this primary zone of people; friends of friends and strangers who hear about the network meeting and want to join it are typically excluded by the original network members. Speck found that approximately forty people could be assembled around lower or middle-class urban white families. Network meetings are settings where changes are brought about by the members of the network with the help of the therapeutic team. Change may also occur between one network meeting and the next as people think over the activities at the meeting and take action. There are three important areas of change: (1) creating a stronger social support system around the individual; (2) decreasing pathology-producing communication patterns in the network; and (3) modifying the life strategies of the labeled person.

Network therapy increases social support around the individual. The network meeting itself mobilizes people to think and act with regard to the troubled person. Later, certain persons in the network may find or provide jobs or housing for the individual; the network meeting mobilizes these resources. Attneave and Speck (1974) suggest that the individual's problems may in part stem from a deteriorated support system and so the network meeting in and of itself is the first step in alleviating this problem. Also, the bonds among people are tightened through the process of participating in the network meeting. The individual's network becomes more cohesive. The therapeutic team facilitates exposing pathological communication patterns, particularly among members of the nuclear schizophrenic family and among them and kin, friends, and neighbors. The team also helps the network to loosen the binds between members of pairs of people. Collusions and secret alliances are systematically exposed. Thus, healthy communications within the social network are increased, while pathologic communications are decreased. The network is designed to "focus on the consequences of the patient's behavior within the network setting for the purpose of enabling the patient to begin to modify and possibly cope differentially with his destructive strategies" (Speck and Rueveni, 1969). Although Attneave and Speck (1974, p. 183) state they do not understand all that goes on in a network meeting, they note that "by simply gathering the network together in one place at one time with the purpose of forming a tighter organization of relationships, potent therapeutic potentials are set in motion."[1] Speck and Rueveni hope that network therapy will be an alternative to hospitalization of the labeled person. Speck (1967) speculates that "in the future, a community network psychotherapy might function as a front line attempt at treatment of problems of persons in a neighborhood."

Attneave (1969) describes a similar type of meeting that occurs naturally in an American Indian tribe to solve interpersonal problems. Attneave uses the concept of *network clan* to refer to the people who are assembled. The concept of network clan combines the closely knit extended family ties based on "inherited and automatically assigned family roles" in the classical sense of the concept of clan, as well as aspects of contemporary urban networks constituted more by group consensus and the active acceptance of relationships by the person at the center of the network. Attneave observed a twenty-four-hour meeting of about fifty people in a network clan to solve the problem of a severely misbehaving six-year-old girl. The girl's mother had married into a network clan organized around the husband's parents, his sisters' families, and their close friends. The young girl had been living with her grandmother for several years and had developed behavior problems. The girl's mother had sent for her and she had become troublesome in the new family, so the network clan convened to solve the problem. This meeting provided a naturally occurring model for the network therapy initiated by Speck and his colleagues.

Speck, Barr, Eisenman, Foulks, Goldman, and Lincoln (1972) intervened in the living situations of youths in "counter-

---

[1] This view of the network meeting in principle contains the basis for our emphasis on the central significance of the general meeting in the Essex network, that is, it is an interpersonally welding force as well as a stimulus to creative thinking about how to take advantage of "opportunities." The introduction of the concept of network into the therapeutic literature is no surprise. Because, beginning with Freud, clinicians became increasingly aware that an individual's behavior was influenced by the obvious fact that he was interconnected in the nuclear, extended, and "work" family. It took a long time for therapists to look beyond the nuclear family network, to become unriveted from an almost exclusive focus on intrapsychic phenomena, and to recognize how the different networks of which an individual was part played a role and, therefore, had to be taken into account in therapeutic tactics and action.

culture" life-style who used drugs. Speck and his colleagues would ask a contact to assemble all the persons he lived with, as well as friends who frequented their "pad." They would name this assemblage a *network* and schedule regular meetings for their research purposes. They found that the youth picked up this label and developed a greater sense of network identity from this experience. In one instance, Speck and his associates entered into an organized political commune that achieved greater identity through the naming, meeting, scheduling, and conceptualization of the researchers. These authors call this change effect *network intervention,* and see this intervention as facilitating counterculture living arrangements in modern urban society. This work became very much based on the value that such forms of network living arrangements were for many people preferable to the traditional nuclear family form of living.

Moreno (1953) describes an intervention on behalf of a girl in a state training school who had emotional and social problems. He used sociometric techniques to trace out the girl's network in the school and explains her likes and dislikes of certain individuals by noting their strategic location in her training school community. Likewise, he explains the widespread dislike of the girl by others as resulting from the diffusion of dislike from two individuals along their networks. He states that she was unable to differentiate between individuals who rejected her directly and those who did so indirectly as a result of the spread of negative feelings through their network. He notes that the network that contributed to her problem was so widespread that it had become almost impossible for her to effect an adjustment on her own. His attempted cure involved changing the structure and dynamics of her network, particularly through influencing key individuals in that network.

Curtis (1974) reported on an extensive project of "team problem solving in a social network." Under the coordination of a state area mental health facility, teams of three to four people, ideally including representatives from state human service agencies and community agencies, and local citizens, were assembled. They acted as coordinators of problem solving in the social network of individuals troublesome to themselves or to others. These teams tackled individuals and their networks who have a broad range of problems and who were referred from many sources. The process was seen as a six-step one. First, the referred individual invites all persons who influenced his problem, both negatively and positively, to the network meeting, but in doing so does not lay blame on any of these people. The idea that each person has an important role in solving the problems is communicated. Second, the problem must be defined. Typically, people are initially reported as the problem, though each person may blame a different individual. The team now takes an active role. "The team's responsibility now is to move the person identified as 'the problem' out of the center and into an equal role with the other network members. The team communicates, in each problem definition, that the individual has a right to have his needs met and that under no circumstances should he simply accept the problem. He should work at resolving it, not at the expense of others but simultaneously with meeting the needs of others. During the process of definition, the sites of conflict are located and legitimate human needs that are being blocked are identified. As the process moves from person-centered to problem-centered, incompatibilities in relationships are separated out for examination, and the restatement increases the alternatives for resolution." Third, resources for change are identified from within the network or are sought from outside the network if necessary. These resources may include medical services and financial support. Fourth, a number of contracts are negotiated between individuals in the network to take concrete steps toward a solution to the defined problems. These first four steps are generally accomplished during the first session.

During the second session, the fifth stage takes place: evaluating the success of the contracts. In this and succeeding meetings, new contracts may be made and new resources may be found, for example, psychotherapy may be initiated if it appears needed. Sixth, the community team terminates their relationship with the network, although this is done in such a way and at such a time as to encourage the network to continue the problem-solving process that has begun. Curtis and his teams have carried out hundreds of such problem-solving interventions in social networks.

Garrison (1974) utilized the social network of people to help them with varying problems at the time of a crisis. He included in the network blood relations, friends, employers, caseworkers, priests, and other service people. Garrison emphasizes the use of a crisis situation in catching a person's social network at a time when he or she is motivated to work for change.

Collins, Emlen, and Watson (1969) and Collins (1973) reported an intervention in natural networks for day-care services, that is, networks of relationships in which individuals seeking nonprofessional day care for their children find it without professional involvement. Typically, there were key helpers in these natural networks, who were in contact with from fifty to seventy-five families and who provided the links between people seeking day-care services and community providers of this service. The professionals located these key people by identifying a population to be served and studying members of that population who had made good adjustments through the help of natural networks and then identifying the key people in their network. The professionals would establish a relationship with these key people for the purpose of helping them increase the numbers of people served and the quality of the service. These people would be advised and supported, but treated as equals to the professional, not put in a paraprofessional role and "trained." Potentially the people actually providing the day care might be offered inputs in day-care programing, health care, or other useful areas.

The six intervention strategies presented represent a broad range of problems and differing ways of focusing on networks. Generally, network intervention provides a way to enter into the broad interpersonal environment that surrounds troubled people. Social network theory provides a way to think about such interventions. It would seem that these strategies are just a beginning; many more strategies for individual change through network intervention might be developed.

Community Intervention Strategies

In our review of the network literature, we uncovered a handful of social scientists who used network conceptualizations to recount or propose actual strategies for community change. These writers are concerned with change in the human services, business, structure and role of government, and change agent's awareness of the network nature of society. In the following discussion, we review the nature of the problems in these four areas and attempted or recommended solutions to them.

The Human Services. Many writers have emphasized that human service institutions are not meeting the needs of community members. Reid and Chandler (1975), for instance, state that "the delivery of human services in most communities suffers from fragmentation, needless overlap and glaring omissions which provide stark evidence of failure in rational management. In such a climate, health, mental health, welfare, educational, and recreational organizations tend to focus on activities relevant to each organization's prestige and power . . . which often impede[s] operating activities." Murrell (1973) observes that the lack of a common source of input into a community's network of human service organizations makes coordination and collaboration among them difficult to achieve. Demone and Harshbarger (1974) stress the need for integrated networks of human service organizations, but note the existence of formidable obstacles to their successful development such as the reality of organizational pluralism, marketplace decisions, the probable unavailability of outside funds and historically characterized bonds and antagonisms between existing organizations. Schön (1971) claims that the "mismatches" between current institutional service arrangements and the societal problems perceived as important increasingly will become "universal" and "endemic."

Many of these writers believe that, as part of the solution to the creation of coordinated, integrated networks of human service organizations, new models of change-oriented organizations must be developed. Schön stresses the importance of establishing an entire "network of organizations and individuals" having contacts with all essential elements of the system being reformed. As an example, he notes that the national system of services for children includes services related to physical health, social welfare, and mental health, and consists of thousands of public and private national, regional, state, and local agencies, each with its own professional and occupational associations, network of laws, administrative regulations, self-interests, pressure groups, and constituencies. Schön states that due to its "multiple-rooted dynamic conservatism," intervention, at a minimum, would need to affect the following: legislators at state and federal levels, administrators of children's agencies at many levels, parents' organizations, middle-level bureaucrats within children's agencies, officials of regulation agencies, innovators or entrepreneurs of new services for children, city and state officials, key figures in relevant professional associations, and media representatives. The structure of the "organization" attempting to reform the system would thus have to be "in the nature of a network mirroring many aspects of the system itself." In addition, he emphasizes that individuals involved in such reform attempts would have to develop unique skills related to negotiating and manipulating network linkages, and utilize extensive interpersonal networks to serve the purposes of both "brokerage" and personal security.

Reid and Chandler (1975) document an attempt to achieve coordination of human service organizations at the community level. A group of human service organizational administrators who had come together to discuss coordination of services for youth decided to enlarge their membership base and broadly redefine their task as one of "identifying diverse needs of target populations and assuming responsibility for planning coordinated programs to meet these ends." Participation was solicited from all local human service organizations, and a "coordinating council" for the town was formed. From the start, it was made clear that commitments to joint programs would be made only by agency administrators, and that only occasional minor resources of mailings would be needed. The larger organizations were asked to appoint representatives from the ranks of their staff (rather than executives) to minimize executive-focused tension in the council. During a three-year period, the council grew to over twenty members, and coordinated six new human service programs and two research studies, in some cases in coordination with the mayor and the town's legislative council. According to Reid and Chandler, the community's human services network has, to date, effectively provided a means to facilitate coordination of services, and minimized the problems of agency competition, regimentation, and duplication of services. The authors record a number of important principles of management that have been helpful in achieving the council's program successes, including the sacrifice of some individual agency priorities, council representation closer to the staff than executive level, equality of membership, a rotating council executive, open discussion of agency mistrust, the recruitment of interested community citizens and agency representatives, and regular verbal and written communication between the council and each agency administrator, to ensure that the executives perceive the council as serving their agency's needs.

Business Sector. A basic problem for business organizations stressed by several writers is that they are increasingly functioning in environments more complex and unpredictable than they can singly deal with. As noted in the section on intraorganizational structures, many organizations have been forced to develop the internal capability to deal effectively with this complex, interorganizational network environment. In addition, some writers recommend that "network organizations" able to aid in the development of coordinated interorganizational networks, and with no vested economic or bureaucratic interests of their own, need to be developed.

Berry, Metcalfe, and McQuillan (1974) claim that the British National Economic Development Office ("Neddy") is an example of such a network organization. They state that Neddy has multiple constituencies but no official authority to intervene or coerce, and no line of formal or informal legitimate power.[2] Neddy deals with unions, business firms, and government agencies, and, according to Berry, Metcalfe, and McQuillan, "seems to be accomplishing results in obtaining positive operations change in these constituent organizations and their environments." They stress that

---

[2] This description of Neddy has some obvious similarities to the Essex network, with one major exception. Neddy is an informal, independent network of organizations, while the Essex network is one of individuals. From our perspective, Neddy deserves the most careful study, precisely because it has no official authority to intervene or coerce, and no line of formal or informal legitimate power. Such a study would also put to the test our belief that an interorganizational network meets unusual constraints precisely because traditional organizational structure seems calculated to prevent rather than to produce change.

Neddy is not part of government nor some sort of research institution, but an organization whose "independent position, flexibility and decentralized structure create a potentiality for acting as an organizational change agent." Its effectiveness depends on its ability to utilize, influence, and develop the interorganizational networks with which it is concerned. The authors contrast the characteristics of network organizations such as Neddy with those of primary "command organizations" (that is, business firms). In addition, Metcalfe (1974) contrasts a network organization with "second-order organizations," whose function it is to "manage whole systems and formulate macropolicies." Metcalfe states that the role of network organizations is to act as a catalyst among the network of second-order organizations, prompting them to recognize their macromanagement responsibilities and promoting cooperation among them. Although the need for such independent network organizations is clear, the authors are not entirely convincing in presenting the reasons why Neddy or other network organizations can succeed where numerous regulatory agencies before them have failed.

The Structure and Role of Government. Schön (1971) presents a radical conceptualization of changes needed in the structure and role of government based on network concepts. He believes that pervasive technological and social changes in contemporary society have dissolved the "stable" basis of the national state, and that as a result national needs will increasingly be changing and policies will become increasingly transient. He claims that neither the rigid, agency-based structure of government, nor its centralized role in the formation and diffusion of policy, can adequately deal with these rapidly changing, locally diverse needs. Agencies developed to deal with certain types of societal issues develop vested interests in the continued importance of those issues, and usually will not adapt to deal with newly evolving problems. New problems and new policies then serve to fragment existing agencies. The diffusion of policy process, in which the federal government identifies societal problems and passes relatively uniform policies to diverse localities, usually fails in solving social problems, because of substantial differences in the perspectives and interests of local agents and the federal government. In addition, the identification of problems and the implementation of new policies usually lags behind local perceptions of real issues. Schön believes that both the structure and role of government must change.

He proposes that structurally the government should move in the direction of organizational flexibility and a capability for continual adaptation by adopting a structure based on "pools of competence" and "task forces." The pools of competence would be organized around specific disciplines or skills. Members from these pools would move in and out of short-lived task forces responsible for specific projects and identify ideally with the federal government, rather than specific departments or agencies. This conceptualization is based on the notion that all levels of governmental employees would be part of cross-cutting, far-reaching, continually shifting networks of societal members.

Schön believes that the "central-periphery" model of the diffusion of policy should yield to a network-based one, in which the movement of policies and ideas is as much from locality to locality, and locality to center (that is, the federal government), as from center to locality. He states that it is at the localities, not at the center, where new problems are likely to be discovered and where experimentation related to the solution of these problems can best occur. Authority would be dispersed within the network, and the role of the federal government would become to detect significant shifts in localities, to pay attention to new ideas and problems as they are identified, and to derive policy themes "by induction." In order for the federal government to play the role of "facilitator of learning" rather than "trainer," extensive networks of people, informally and highly interconnected, would need to be utilized. Schön (1974) details an example in which government changed from a central-periphery stance to a more network-oriented one. The Regional Medical Program, devised in the mid-1960s, had as its goal the adoption by local medical systems a mode of regionalization of medical care based on the linkage of every center of medical teaching and research to a periphery of community hospitals and practicing physicians. The federal commission involved had 100 million dollars to distribute to regions, and was responsible for overseeing, controlling, and evaluating the diffusion of the model throughout fifty-five regions. The actual goals of the local regions, however, turned out to be different than those of the federal government, and several local coordinators successfully used the money to begin transforming the local medical networks in ways they thought most important. Meanwhile, federal priorities were changing, and a new goal of achieving transformation of medical networks by encouraging the voluntary rearrangements of existing institutions emerged as dominant. The Regional Medical Program seemed the best vehicle to carry this out, yet the realization emerged that, due to the diversity of regional starting conditions and problems, no general model for systems transformation could be offered. Officials decided to leave each region free to devise its own policies for change and to institute its own evaluation system. The federal government's role had shifted from the imposition of specific policies to an enunciation of general themes. According to Schön, central policy was now inductively derived from regions, and the federal government was in a position to connect regions to one another and produce a "network for learning" about transformations of the medical system.

Schön (1974) claims that in order to adapt successfully to the rapidly changing nature of society we must be able to "learn about . . . situation[s] while we are in them . . . and to organize action so that we learn through the action we undertake." Government, the major societal institution responsible for public learning, plays the crucial role in this process. In order to best fulfill this role, Schön believes, government must become adept at the design, development and management of networks—an internal network structure, an external network of learning-oriented localities, and an extensive, highly interconnected network of people critical to the effective functioning of the internal and external networks.

Change Agent Awareness. Sarason (1976a) believes that a major factor involved in the failure of many efforts at change has been that interveners have lacked a realistic awareness of the interconnectedness of the organization that is being changed with a complex network of other organizations.

> One of the most frequent mistakes that is made
> is to neglect or vastly underestimate the importance of
> answering these questions: What individuals or groups

will be directly affected by the proposed program? What issues of territoriality will it raise for which agencies, professions, and other interest groups? Who can be counted on to put obstacles in the way of the proposed program? Who has the power, actual or potential, to prematurely terminate the program? When you try systematically to answer these and related questions—and these questions refer to one's own organization as well as to external ones—you will find that what you propose to do impinges on networks radiating far into the community, that is, that what you propose to do will become related to quite an array of existing relationships. Indeed, performing this exercise is instructive in giving one a healthy appreciation of the myriads of interlocking networks that exist in a community. Unfortunately, an appreciation of this has always come *after* the program has failed, or has been aborted, or has fallen far short of the mark, or has been so transformed that its original goals are no longer in the picture. But even that is a too charitable assessment, because in many instances the major "lesson" articulated is that there are a lot of stupid, selfish, power-hungry people in the community who feed on well-intentioned, health-giving professionals.

There is a problem in dealing with these questions that can easily be overlooked (it almost always is), and once stated it is "obvious." Those who conceive the program, passionate and committed to a set of substantive ideas they consider innovative and needed, are not in the best psychological set to deal ahead of time with the radiating community consequences of their program. They are psychologically in a set in which optimism and hope and possession of their version of the truth obliterate a systematic approach to the question. In my experience, even when there is a sensitive awareness to these questions, one can predict that they will encounter in themselves two sources of resistance. The first is that it will take time, more time than they are willing or prepared to give. The second source is that, as they tap into existing networks to get soundings, they are likely to find—they will always find—nodes of opposition. They are, in fact, likely to find that their ideas can be expected

to galvanize existing networks, near and far, in opposition
to their program. Even if their proposal is to give away
large sums of money to afflicted individuals or community
agencies—to ask nothing of the community but to accept
the money—they will encounter all sorts of opposition
and criticism.

It is apparent, I hope, that in raising questions
about consequences I have been leading up to the crucial
point that a community venture requires support, the
kind of support that one can count on to surmount the
numerous obstacles that the answers to the questions
indicated. And that is the point: The process of tapping
into networks to obtain information and soundings is the
first stage of the process of answering the question: How
much support will we require from what networks to
provide us with a fighting chance? And the chances are
always fighting ones. It is beyond the scope of this article
to pursue the processes of gaining support and the
dilemmas of compromise. I wish to conclude this part
of my presentation by emphasizing that the root cause
of the failures I have observed inheres in a conception of
a community that ill prepared us for understanding its
complexity and our actual and potential relationships to
it, as well as for harnessing its resources behind our efforts.

Implicit in Sarason's observations is the idea that conceptions of the
dynamics of action and change imply conceptions of the nature of
human networks and not until the two conceptions are integrated
will the fruitfulness and validity of either conception be established.
At the very least, his observations suggest that the continued isolation from each other of conceptions of action and networks raises
considerably the odds against successful actions for change.

12

Settings, Networks,
and Resources

ⳡⳡⳡⳡⳡⳡⳡⳡⳡⳡⳡⳡⳡⳡⳡ

We become aware of a social change after it has already begun to take place, and that awareness in turn tends to accelerate the pace of change. But the substance of social change has many faces, if only because different individuals and groups interpret, react, or accommodate to the change in different ways. Our labels and language give to the change the appearance of a coherence and direction it rarely deserves. Regardless of whether we are for or against the change, we tend to see its antecedents and consequences rather narrowly, that is, as if the change had the characteristics of a "thing." We can look at the current social scene and research literature and conclude that a change is taking place in how individuals, groups, and organizations (private and public) view the quality and quantity of the networks of which they are a part. The word *network*, as well as concepts of networks, is increasing dramatically in use and as a focus of interest and action. Nowhere is this more true than in local, state, and federal governments where public officials struggle to forge new connections among agencies, departments, and programs in the attempt to make the boundaries among them more permeable. Not infrequently, this struggle culminates in a defeat hidden by the creation of a new vehicle whose stated function is to "coordinate," to establish cross-agency networks of relationships, not only to eliminate "waste," but also to make more relevant resources available to each of the agencies. Almost always, these resources are in the form of information and no sharing beyond that takes place, the result being that the gulf between appearance and reality has not been bridged. The scope and difficulty of the problem are exponentially increased when it is seen that what is troublesome within government is no less so in regard to the myriad community groups, agencies, and programs receiving governmental support. It is here that we find the word *network* increasingly being used. For example, at a recent conference on aging, federal and state officials emphasized that what was being (and *had* to be) developed was a network of services for the elderly. And, in fact, several states had rather elaborate exhibits describing their "network of services." The complexity of one exhibit can be imagined by noting that well over five hundred discrete agencies and programs were part of the network. The graphic presentation was, of course, quite impressive, but, as more than a few participants noted, there was little correspondence between what the graphic portrayal intended to convey and the actual nature of the network interconnections. It would be unfair to impute evil intent to anyone, because that would suggest that in using a fashionable label like *network* these public officials meant more than (1) there were many agencies and programs serving the elderly, (2) these agencies had an obligation to be aware of each other, and (3) in some instances some of these agencies were responsible to a coordinating central or regional council. This is a network; but there are networks and there are networks. On what basis, then, can one fault their use of their concept of a network? The answer is that at the same time that every agency is agonizingly aware of a discrepancy between its resources and what it feels it should be doing, that type of network does not really speak to their problem. They hope it does, and in some minimal way it may, but not enough to change their level of frustration. In a real sense, it is a legislated network with money as an incentive and controls (implicit and explicit) as a consequence. We have discussed in Chapter Five one of the most ambitious federal attempts to forge such a network and, if the unfortunate fate of that program is any guide, one cannot be optimistic about legislated networks.

On the most general level, one must ask if an Essex-type network is viable within and under the aegis of a complicated formal organization, public or private. This question has to be raised, because we can expect in the coming years that, as our society is forced to confront the fact of limited resources, the concept of network will increasingly and explicitly be applied to efforts aimed at more efficient use of resources. If the likelihood is high that these efforts will only prove that the more things change the more they remain the same, we should, at the very least, try to avoid participating uncritically in a "movement" whose goals are as virtuous as its fruitfulness is suspect. We do not say this as cynics or prophets of gloom, or because the answer to our question has an empirical base, but rather to suggest that the important question is: What conditions have to exist to permit an Essex-type network to be viable in a traditional, complicated, formal organization? The very form of the question suggests that these conditions will not be frequently found. Let us illustrate the point on the basis of an unpublished manuscript in which is described in some detail an apparently successful effort to develop an Essex-type network in a school system. We are grateful to William Fibkins for allowing us to see the manuscript.[1] It is important to note that what he describes took place independent of any knowledge of the Essex network.

We cannot do justice to Fibkins' account: its detail, personal quality, and personal and organizational history. We shall attempt only to state succinctly a few of the highlights.

1. Pervading the account is a sensitivity to the loneliness of teachers and its consequences for morale, resistance to change, and student discontent. This sensitivity extends

---

[1] Fibkins is a school counselor and project director of the Bay Shore-Stony Brook Teacher Center on Long Island in New York. The manuscript, a draft of an untitled book that hopefully will be published, became available to us after our book was almost in final form.

to the plight of teachers' "midcareer crisis": flagging interest, psychological withdrawal from students, and crippling feelings of isolation.

2. There is a description of numerous efforts (federal, state, local) to help teachers, none of which had more than a temporary effect.

3. Fibkins concludes that common to all of these efforts was the failure to give teachers and others a sense of meaningful participation in decision making. Also, he comes to see that within any school or school system there are many resources that are untapped but potentially available in the most personally and organizationally productive ways. And, by *resources*, he means more than "professionals"; for example, he includes secretaries and janitors.

4. He also comes to see that the process whereby these resources will be recognized and utilized would have to be based on voluntary participation. That is to say, as long as people do not believe that they have something to gain by participation, they cannot give their resources to others who may need them. There has to be, in our terms, a give-and-get relationship.

5. Fibkins recognized that what was needed was an informal, voluntary association in a formal organization, but he feared the pressures to become formal and to accommodate to existing organizational practices and traditions: the very things that made change and innovation almost impossible. He was also aware that he had to avoid getting caught in the cross-fire between the teacher union and "management."

The result was a "teachers' center" located in the district junior high school. The flavor and substance of the center are best described in Fibkins' own words:

At the present time the center operates *daily* workshops with emphasis on meeting the changing needs of a staff that will probably live out their professional careers in this setting. We are no longer associated with a university, because of the economic "crunch" that has hit the schools very hard. Yet we are creatively "alive" in the sense that the staff has come forward to supplement the consultant cost of our university person out of their own pockets. Their generous donations have made it possible for us to continue this liaison. My own salary continues to be supported by the district. In terms of "expansion," we have found that it is very difficult to duplicate our setting in other schools in the district. Each school has its own dynamics, and it seems inappropriate for us to say that what is good for this school is good for another. Elementary teachers seem to have far less time to interact with each other, while high school staff seem to be still suffering from the depression of the student confrontations of the late 60's. Still there is always the pressure on us to "expand," even though our own learnings about renewal programs suggest very strongly that, whenever possible, this process should go on in the building in which the teacher works, and centers be staffed by people who are known and trusted by the staff. In our school culture one simply cannot expect most teachers to venture to "strange lands" after school to take part in workshops, etc. Nor can one expect the staff development specialist from the "strange land," whether it be a university or nearby junior high, to come to the teacher's setting and involve that teacher with any degree of permanence. No staff development specialist can physically or emotionally expect to work in developing more than one setting at a time. And this work takes time—years. One solution would be to utilize teachers who might be excessed and train them for staff development roles. Clearly, the need and resources are there to create these new settings. It takes more piloting, more doing, to demonstrate the many different kinds of approaches that are possible.

We have also survived a contract year, in which the center was able to maintain its neutral position between management and unions. We personally entered into the struggle on the part of the union as union members, yet worked to keep the center territory neutral and a place for everyone to attend, from the Superintendent to union members. . . .

As our process evolved, staff seemed more sure of themselves with students and were interested in experiencing "different" kinds of learning now available to them. Whereas prior to the teachers' center, teachers on the staff were known only for their subject matter, now teachers could view the school community staff as 130 different people, with different skills, interests, experiences—all of which could be used in their own development as a "learner" and also with students. Learning could now be viewed in a broad network that included all the personnel in the school district, community, local universities, libraries, and national resources such as the School of the Future at the University of Massachusetts. In a very definite way, we had begun to change the "way" in which the learning process was viewed in the school. When staff needs emerged, staff development people could help staff to think in terms of the "learning" concept suggested by Illich; that is, to consider the total environment for resources to meet their needs. One need not limit oneself to the department chairman, principal, and university for resources. The community contained many exciting "teachers"—musicians, artists, painters, writers, artisans, craftsmen, and philosophers of every persuasion. The learning network was there to use. All we had to do was ask.

It can be tentatively suggested, then, that the center process helped to move teachers who Thelen describes as "Tradesmen-teachers" (those who see inservice education as a place to find particular weapons or tools to use) more into the role of "cathedral-builders"; that is, to become teachers who see their own education as a way to spontaneously create appropriate structures of response to the varying demands of their daily work. We have found that the "tradesman" does indeed have the soul of an artist—he can be spontaneous, creative, given the opportunity to experience new and different ways to learn and to know this part of himself over a period of time. The search for "tools of the trade" in renewal is only a mask to cover up the fears and anxieties we feel in confronting 130 different faces and personalities each day. We can load up our closets with gimmicks, keep the students working at a furious pace—but if we fail to confront the essential loneliness of our profession, that we need to share with others, to learn from others—we will only increase our loneliness. For, after all is said and done, the most important part of any renewal process is to help the "teacher"—whether he be teacher, administrator, secretary, teacher aide, custodian, to "ask," and to be "heard" by someone. The most important role of the staff development person is to encourage the "other" to speak out loud, in his own words, his fears, concerns, and to state "I need this now to help me get through the day—to feel more the power I know I have as a person." For teaching is a lonely activity, always giving away of oneself. To ask for something for oneself is foreign to the way we usually do things in the school.

Fibkins' account demonstrates that an Essex-type network can be successfully developed within a traditional, formal institution. But, as he points out, it does not follow that a similar teacher center would flourish in many other school districts. Indeed, in recounting the prehistory of the center, Fibkins says:

Another important aspect of the beginning step toward developing a renewal center relates to the ease with which we were able to initiate the inservice course. We approached the principal, assistant superintendent, and teachers in the building and received a very supportive response. Part of this was due to the fact that historically the district had always been a first-rate school district, and there existed an atmosphere in which change could happen. Though the turmoils of the late 60's had put a damper on some of this enthusiasm, there still existed a basis for the notion that the district had capable teachers and good programs. Why did this school district so easily support a teacher-initiated program, while in a neighboring district a colleague attempted to do the same thing and spent a fruitless year listing

goals, purposes, and going through faculty councils? In
the end he just caved in under the weight of the paper-
work and time required to justify his program.

But Fibkins' entire account has one major significance that
requires us to withhold judgment about the applicability of his
efforts to other school districts. One does not need his account to
predict that any meaningful innovation will "take" in a few settings,
will be subverted or inappropriately transformed in most settings,
and will be rejected outright in a few. The question his account
raises, and it is one we discussed repeatedly in our account of the
Essex network, centers around the leader's style and thinking.

Again the Mrs. Dewar Issue

When we read Fibkins' manuscript, we had something akin
to a déjà vu experience. In terms of the substance and development
of his thinking, and his personal style, as far as that can be inferred
from his writing, his similarities to Mrs. Dewar are remarkable.
What is heartening is the confirmation the similarities provide for
our contention that Mrs. Dewar's achievements could not be solely
or even primarily attributed to her affluence or community status.
The social soil into which an individual attempts to plant and
nurture the seeds of change is undoubtedly fateful for what will
grow. To underestimate the significance of this factor borders on
the ridiculous. And yet, it is no less a mistake to underestimate the
power of the right combination of style and conceptual substance.
The reader will recall that in Chapter Nine we discussed a high
school principal who, in terms of style and determination, could
have done, we believed, what Mrs. Dewar did. But he lacked that
conceptual substance and orientation without which he and his
colleagues would remain mired in frustration as they saw the gulf
between their pitiful resources and their myriad problems remain
constant and overwhelming. We cannot say what would happen if
more people like Fibkins achieved his conceptual clarity, a clarity
that brought together values, concepts, and a penetrating understanding of the culture of his setting.[2] It is a clarity that speaks to

[2] After this book was already in press, we became aware of the

what people feel, and calls forth from them a positive response. We cannot say how many people like Fibkins and Mrs. Dewar there are. But we cannot allow disillusionment with past efforts at change, and cynicism about future possibilities, to drag us into a passivity or nihilism that robs living of purpose. The malaise that has set in as a reaction to the reform movements of the sixties may be understandable, but it is far from being as justifiable as some would have us believe. After all, if these movements fell far short of their mark, it implicates, among other things, our conceptual naiveté. If we find that our world did not bend to our efforts, that says a good deal about our world, but it also says something about ourselves and our ideas. These thoughts do not stem either from a Panglossian stance about possible futures or from the security that we have learned all we needed to learn. What does concern us is that the use of the word *network* and the concept of network are becoming increasingly fashionable. They are "in the air" and that suggests they speak to something important in the lives of people. It is realistic and not pessimistic to expect that some people will view "networking" as a panacea and devise "methods" by which the new gospel will be spread. Efforts at social change never wait on proof that the values and ideas powering the efforts have validity. If "networking" takes on some of the characteristics of a movement, we have cause to be fearful and optimistic, fearful because we know the consequences of unbridled enthusiasm and simple answers, and optimistic that perhaps on balance there will be a desirable difference. There are alternatives to optimism, but they have no place in an Essex-type network.

---

accomplishments of Daphne Krause, executive director, Minneapolis Age and Opportunity Center, Inc. The rationale she describes, the examples she provides, and the scale of her network-organizational activities are given in "Hearing before the Subcommittee on Health and Long-Term Care of the Select Committee on Aging, House of Representatives, ninety-fourth congress (First Session), July 8, 1975." (Available from Superintendent of Documents, U.S. Government Printing Office, Washington, D.C. 20402. Stock number 052–070–02903–0. Price $1.70.) The similarities between Ms. Krause, Mrs. Dewar, and Dr. Fibkins are startling, except that Ms. Krause's accomplishments are on a much vaster scale. The reader is urged to read her extended testimony to grasp the fruitfulness of a rationale almost identical to that of the Essex network.

References

AIKEN, M., AND ALFORD, A. "Community Structure and Innovation: The Case for Urban Renewal." *American Sociological Review*, 1970, *35*, 650–652.

ATTNEAVE, C. L. "Therapy in Tribal Settings and Urban Network Intervention." *Family Process*, 1969, *8*, 192–210.

ATTNEAVE, C. L., AND SPECK, R. V. "Social Network Intervention in Time and Space." In A. Jacobs and W. W. Spradlin (Eds.), *The Group as Agent of Change: Treatment, Prevention, Personal Growth in the Family, the School, the Mental Hospital and the Community*. New York: Behavioral Publications, 1974.

BAKER, F., AND SCHULBERG, H. "Community Health Caregiving Systems." In A. Sheldon, F. Baker, and C. McLaughlin (Eds.), *Systems and Medical Care*. Cambridge, Mass.: MIT Press, 1970.

189

BARKER, R. G. *Ecological Psychology: Concepts and Methods for Studying the Environment of Human Behavior.* Palo Alto, Calif.: Stanford University Press, 1968.

BARKER, R. G., AND GUMP, P. V. *Big School, Small School: High School Size and Student Behavior.* Palo Alto, Calif.: Stanford University Press, 1964.

BARNES, J. A. "Class and Committees in a Norwegian Island Parish." *Human Relations,* 1954, *7,* 39–58.

BARRETT, W. *Irrational Man: A Study in Existential Philosophy.* New York: Doubleday, 1962.

BECKER, M. "Sociometric Location and Innovativeness." *American Sociological Review,* 1970, *35,* 267–282.

BENSON, J. K. "The Interorganizational Network as a Political Economy." *Administrative Science Quarterly,* 1975, *20,* 229–249.

BERRY, D. F., METCALFE, L., AND MCQUILLAN, W. " 'Neddy'—An Organizational Metamorphosis." *Journal of Management Studies,* 1974, *11,* 1–20.

BIGELOW, D. N. *The Liberal Arts and Teacher Education.* Lincoln, Neb.: University of Nebraska Press, 1971.

BOISSEVAIN, J. "An Exploration of Two First-Order Zones." In J. Boissevain and J. C. Mitchell (Eds.), *Network Analysis: Studies in Human Interaction.* Mouton, Netherlands: Mouton, 1973.

BOISSEVAIN, J. *Friends of Friends.* Oxford: Blackwell, 1974.

BOSWELL, D. M. "Personal Crisis and the Mobilization of the Social Network." In J. C. Mitchell (Ed.), *Social Networks in Urban Situations: Analyses of Personal Relationships in Central African Towns.* Manchester, England: Manchester University Press, 1969.

BOTT, E. *Family and Social Networks.* London: Tavistock, 1957.

BURNS, T., AND STALKER, G. M. *The Management of Innovation.* London: Tavistock, 1961.

CAPLAN, G. *Support Systems and Community Mental Health.* New York: Behavioral Publications, 1974.

CLARK, T. N. *Community Power and Policy Outputs: A Review of Urban Research.* Beverly Hills, Calif.: Sage, 1973.

COLEMAN, J., KATZ, E., AND MENZEL, H. "The Diffusion of an Innovation Among Physicians." *Sociometry,* 1957, *20,* 253–270.

COLEMAN, J., KATZ, E., AND MENZEL, H. *Medical Innovation: A Diffusion Study.* Indianapolis: Bobbs-Merrill, 1966.

COLEMAN, J. S., AND OTHERS. *Equality of Educational Opportunity.* Superintendent of Documents Catalog No. FS 5.238:38001.

Washington, D.C.: U.S. Government Printing Office, Department of Health, Education and Welfare, 1966.

COLLINS, A. H. "Natural Delivery Systems: Accessible Sources of Power for Mental Health." *American Journal of Orthopsychiatry,* 1973, *43,* 46–52.

COLLINS, A. H., EMLEN, A., AND WATSON, E. "The Day-Care Neighbor Service: An Interventive Experiment." *Community Mental Health Journal,* 1969, *5,* 219–224.

CRAVEN, P., AND WELLMAN, B. "The Network City." *Sociological Inquiry,* 1973, *43,* 57–88.

CROOG, S. H., LIPSON, A., AND LEVINE, S. "Help Patterns in Severe Illness: The Role of Kin Network, Non-Family Resources and Institutions." *Journal of Marriage and the Family,* 1972, *34,* 32–41.

CURTIS, W. R. "Team Problem Solving in a Social Network." *Psychiatric Annals,* 1974, *4,* 11–27.

CURTIS, R. L., JR., AND ZURCHER, L. A. "Stable Resources of Protest Movements: The Multiorganizational Field." *Social Forces,* 1973, *52,* 53–61.

DEMONE, H. W., JR., AND HARSHBARGER, D. *A Handbook for Human Service Organizations.* New York: Behavioral Publications, 1974.

EMERY, F. E., AND TRIST, E. L. "The Causal Texture of Organizational Environments." *Human Relations,* 1965, *18,* 21–32.

EPSTEIN, A. L. "The Network and Urban Social Organization." *Rhodes-Livingstone Journal,* 1961, *29,* 29–62.

EVAN, W. M. "The Organization-Set: Toward a Theory of Interorganizational Relations." In J. D. Thompson (Ed.), *Approaches to Organizational Design.* Pittsburgh: University of Pittsburgh Press, 1966.

EVAN, W. M. "Multinational Corporations and International Professional Associations." *Human Relations,* 1974, *27,* 587–625.

FIBKINS, W. Unpublished Manuscript. Bay Shore Junior High School (Guidance Department), 393 Brook Ave., Bay Shore, N.Y. 11706.

FROST, C. F. "Keynote Address to the Labor-Management Conference." Paper presented at the Labor-Management Conference, New York, October 20, 1976. (Available from author at the Department of Psychology, Michigan State University, East Lansing, Mich.)

GANS, H. *The Urban Villagers.* New York: Free Press, 1962.

GARRISON, J. "Network Techniques: Case Studies in the Screening-

Linking-Planning Conference Method." *Family Process,* 1974, *13,* 337–353.

GARTNER, A., KOHLER, M., AND RIESSMAN, F. *Children Teach Children: Learning by Teaching.* New York: Harper & Row, 1971.

GIBSON, G. "Kin Family Network: Overheralded Structure in Past Conceptualizations of Family Functioning." *Journal of Marriage and the Family,* 1972, *39,* 13–23.

GRANOVETTER, M. S. "Changing Jobs: Channels of Mobility Information in a Suburban Community." Unpublished doctoral dissertation, Harvard University, 1970.

GRANOVETTER, M. S. "The Strength of Weak Ties." *American Journal of Sociology,* 1973, *78,* 1360–1380.

HAGE, J. *Communication and Organizational Control: Cybernetics in Health and Welfare Settings.* New York: Wiley, 1974.

HAMMER, M. "Influence of Small Social Networks as Factors in Mental Hospital Admission." *Human Organization,* 1964, *22,* 243–251.

HEBERT, H., AND MURPHY, E. *Network Analysis: A Selected Bibliography.* Exchange Bibliography No. 165. Monticello, Ill.: Council of Planning Librarians, 1970.

HENRY, J. "The Personal Community and Its Invariant Properties." *American Anthropologist,* 1958, *60,* 827–831.

JONGMAN, D. G. "Politics and the Village Level." In J. Boissevain and J. C. Mitchell (Eds.), *Network Analysis: Studies in Human Interaction.* Mouton, Netherlands: Mouton, 1973.

KATZ, W., AND LAZARSFELD, P. F. *Personal Influence: The Part Played by People in the Flow of Mass Communications.* Glencoe, Ill.: Free Press, 1955.

KINGDON, D. R. *Matrix Organizations: Managing Information Technologies.* London: Tavistock, 1973.

KORTE, C., AND MILGRAM, S. "Acquaintance Networks Between Racial Groups." *Journal of Personality and Social Psychology,* 1970, *15,* 101–108.

LAUMANN, E. O. *Bonds of Pluralism: The Form and Substance of Urban Society.* New York: Wiley, 1973.

LAUMANN, E. O., AND PAPPI, F. U. "New Directions in the Study of Community Elites." *American Sociological Review,* 1973, *38,* 212–230.

LEE, N. H. *The Search for an Abortionist.* Chicago: University of Chicago Press, 1969.

LEICHTER, H. J., AND MITCHELL, W. E. *Kinship and Casework.* New York: Russell Sage Foundation, 1967.

LEKACHMAN, R. "The Poverty of Influence." *Commentary*, 1970, *49*, 39–44.

LEVINE, J. "The Sphere of Influence." *American Sociological Review*, 1972, *37*, 14–27.

LEVINE, M., AND LEVINE, A. *A Social History of Helping Services*. New York: Appleton-Century-Crofts, 1970.

LIBERMAN, R. "Personal Influence in the Use of Mental Health Resources." *Human Organization*, 1965, *24*, 231–235.

MAYER, A. C. "System and Network: An Approach to the Study of Political Process in Dewas." In T. Madan and G. Sarana (Eds.), *Indian Anthropology: Essays in Memory of D. N. Majumdar*. Bombay: Asia Publishing House, 1962.

MAYER, A. C. "The Significance of Quasi-Groups in the Study of Complex Societies." In M. Banton (Ed.), *The Social Anthropology of Complex Societies*. Association of Social Anthropologists Monograph No. 4. New York: Praeger, 1966.

MCKINLAY, J. B. "Social Networks, Lay Consultation, and Help-Seeking Behavior." *Social Forces*, 1973, *51*, 275–292.

MERRENS, M. R. "Nonemergency Helping Behavior in Various-Sized Communities." *Journal of Social Psychology*, 1973, *90*, 327–328.

MERROW, J., FOSTER, R., AND ESTES, N. *The Urban School Superintendent of the Future*. Durant, Okla.: Southeastern Foundation, 1974.

MERTON, R. *Social Theory and Social Structure* (Rev. ed.). Glencoe, Ill.: Free Press, 1957.

METCALFE, J. L. "Systems Models, Economic Models and the Texture of Organizational Environments: An Approach to Macroorganization Theory." *Human Relations*, 1974, *27*, 639–664.

MILGRAM, S. "The Small-World Problem." *Psychology Today*, 1967, *1*, 62–67.

MITCHELL, J. C. "The Concept and Use of Social Networks." In J. C. Mitchell (Ed.), *Social Networks in Urban Situations: Analyses of Personal Relationships in Central African Towns*. Manchester, England: Manchester University Press, 1969.

MORENO, J. L. *Who Shall Survive? A New Approach to the Study of Human Interrelations*. Washington, D.C.: Nervous and Mental Disease Publishing, 1934.

MORENO, J. L. *Who Shall Survive? Foundations of Sociometry, Group Psychotherapy and Sociodrama*. Beacon, N.Y.: Beacon House, 1953.

MURRELL, S. A. *Community Psychology and Social Systems.* New York: Behavioral Publications, 1973.

NISBET, R. A. *Social Change and History.* New York: Oxford University Press, 1969.

PERRUCCI, R., AND PILISUK, M. "Leaders and Ruling Elites: The Interorganization Bases of Community Power." *American Sociological Review,* 1970, *35,* 1040–1057.

President's Science Advisory Committee, Panel on Youth. *Youth: Transition to Adulthood.* Washington, D.C.: U.S. Government Printing Office, 1973.

PROVUS, M. M. *The Grand Experiment.* Berkeley, Calif.: McCutchan, 1975.

REID, T. A., AND CHANDLER, G. E. The Evolution of a Human Services Network. Hamden, Conn.: Hamden Mental Health Service, 1975. (Mimeographed)

ROGERS, E. M., AND SHOEMAKER, F. F. *Communication of Innovations: A Cross-Cultural Approach* (2nd ed.). New York: Free Press, 1971.

SARASON, S. B. *The Psychological Sense of Community: Prospects for a Community Psychology.* San Francisco: Jossey-Bass, 1974.

SARASON, S. B. "Community Psychology, Networks, and Mr. Everyman." *American Psychologist,* 1976a, *31,* 317–328.

SARASON, S. B. "Educational Policy and Federal Intervention in the Days of Opportunity." *Journal of Education,* Boston University, 1976b.

SARASON, S. B. *Work, Aging, and Social Change: Professionals and the One Life-One Career Imperative.* New York: Free Press, 1977.

SAUNDERS, J. T., AND REPPUCCI, N. D. "Learning Networks Among Administrators of Human Service Institutions." *American Journal of Community Psychology,* in press.

SCHÖN, D. A. *Beyond the Stable State.* New York: Random House, 1971.

SCHÖN, D. A. "The Technology of Public Learning." 1974. (Mimeographed.)

SHAPIRO, J. "Dominant Leaders Among Slum Hotel Residents." *American Journal of Orthopsychiatry,* 1969, *39,* 644–650.

SHULMAN, N. "Urban Social Networks." Unpublished doctoral dissertation, University of Toronto, 1972.

SPECK, R. V. "Psychotherapy of the Social Network of a Schizophrenic Family." *Family Process,* 1967, *6,* 208–214.

SPECK, R. V., BARR, J., EISENMAN, R., FOULKS, E., GOLDMAN, A., AND LINCOLN, J. *The New Families.* New York: Basic Books, 1972.

SPECK, R. V., AND REUVENI, V. "Network Therapy—A Developing Concept." *Family Process,* 1969, *8,* 182–190.

SUSSMAN, M. B., AND BURCHINAL, L. "Parental Aid to Married Children: Implications for Family Functioning." *Marriage and Family Living,* 1962, *24,* 320–332.

THOMPSON, R. A. "A Theory of Instrumental Social Networks." *Journal of Anthropological Research,* 1973, *29,* 244–254.

TILLY, C., AND BROWN, H. C. "On Uprooting, Kinship and the Auspices of Migration." *International Journal of Comparative Sociology,* 1967, *8,* 139–164.

TOLSDORF, C. "Social Networks and the Coping Process." Amherst, Mass.: University of Massachusetts, 1975. (Mimeographed.)

TURK, H. "Interorganizational Networks in Urban Society: Initial Perspectives and Comparative Research." *American Sociological Review,* 1970, *35,* 1–19.

WALTON, J. "Substance and Artifact: The Current Status on Research of Community Power Structure." *American Journal of Sociology,* 1966, *71,* 430–438.

WARREN, R. "The Interorganizational Field as a Focus for Investigation." *Administrative Science Quarterly,* 1967, *12,* 396–419.

WICKER, A. W. "Undermanning Theory and Research: Implications for the Study of Psychological and Behavioral Effects of Excess Populations." *Representative Research in Social Psychology,* 1973, *4,* 185–206.

WICKER, A. W., AND KIRMEYER, S. "From Church to Laboratory to National Park." In S. Wapner, S. B. Cohen, and B. Kaplan (Eds.), *Experiencing the Environment.* New York: Plenum Press, 1976.

Index

A

Abortion networks, 133-134
Administrative Sciences, 9, 126
Agency-agency relationships, 41
AIKEN, M., 140, 189
ALFORD, A., 140, 189
American Medical Association, 16
Anthropology, 4, 9, 126, 132, 135
ATTNEAVE, C. L., 165, 166, 167, 189

B

BAKER, F., 139, 189
BANTON, M., 193
BARKER, R. G., 117, 118, 119, 190
BARNES, J. A., 11, 132, 135, 190

BARR, J., 12, 167, 194
BARRETT, W., 25, 190
Barter economy, 21, 27, 50, 60
Bay Shore Stony Brook Teacher
    Center, 181
BECKER, M., 161, 190
BENSON, J. K., 139, 190
BERRY, D. F., 173, 190
Beyond the Stable State (Schön), 143
BIGELOW, D., 5, 67, 68, 69, 70, 72, 76,
    190
BOISSEVAIN, J., 135, 190, 192
BOSWELL, D. M., 162, 163, 190
BOTT, E., 10, 134, 135, 190
BROWN, H. C., 133, 195
BURCHINAL, L., 12, 136, 195
BURNS, T., 13, 142, 143, 190

197